BEGINNINGS

Betty Jane Wylie

BEGINNINGS
A Book for Widows

McClelland and Stewart

ISBN: 0-7710-9057-9 (hardcover)
   0-7710-9058-7 (paperback)

The Canadian Publishers
McClelland and Stewart Limited
25 Hollinger Road, Toronto M4B 3G2

The author and publisher gratefully acknowledge the assistance of The Canadian Life Insurance Association in making this book possible.

Printed and bound in Canada

CANADIAN CATALOGUING IN PUBLICATION DATA
Wylie, Betty Jane, 1931-
   Beginnings
Bibliography: p.
ISBN 0-7710-9057-9 bd.   ISBN 0-7710-9058-7 pa.
1. Widows   I. Title.
HQ1058.W94   301.42'86   C77-001359-7

Contents

Acknowledgements

This is a book that had to be written. It takes time to learn to be a wife. Perhaps it takes equal time to learn to be a widow, longer, because there's no one to help you learn. It is a more painful process and it is singular.

Because I am by nature a communicative person I have expressed some of my feelings about the process, most publicly in *Maclean's* magazine. I'd like to thank all the widows and widowers who responded to me and whose comments I have quoted in these pages.

I'd also like to thank The Canadian Life Insurance Association, who originally commissioned a guide for widows and then helped me expand it into a book, and Jonathyn Forbes, formally of Marshall Fenn Limited, who conceived the project for the CLIA and guided me in its initial stages. I have received valuable help and advice and information all along the way but special thanks go to Joseph J.R. Sheehan, CLU, and Mary Vachon, mental health consultant to the Clarke Institute.

for Bill

BEGINNINGS

1

The end and the beginning

It isn't for the moment you are struck that you need courage, but for the long uphill climb back to sanity and faith and security.

Anne Morrow Lindbergh

"Every beginning is hard," states a German proverb, and this is no exception. To begin a book with an ending is no way to begin, but this is where you and I come in.

There is no faster way to stop a conversation than to give a straight answer to someone you have just met who asks you, "Where is your husband?" At the moment of truth, the questioner indicates that he wishes the floor would open up and swallow him, and both of you are left at a loss for words. But you might as well get on with it.

Here goes.

My husband was a healthy, vigorous man who took good care of himself. We both worked out three or four times a week at a health club; we watched our weight – he more successfully than I – and we had yearly checkups. At his most recent check-up Bill had been pronounced in excellent condition, cholesterol count low, recovery time good. He was forty-five years old, six foot three, and weighed 175 pounds. On our regular walks we were beginning to look forward to an active old age together. In short, if he were alive today, he'd be a very healthy man.

He burped shortly after Easter Sunday dinner in April, 1973, and died. Death by asphyxiation: the valve in his epiglottis failed to close again after the slight regurgitation, and food got into his windpipe, thence into his lungs and suffocated him within about eight minutes. He didn't know what hit him. Neither did we.

It is not as freaky a death as it might seem; there are statistics on it, and magazine articles are beginning to tell how to prevent such a death. Apparently it is more preventable if food lodges in the windpipe going down than if it sticks there on its way back up. That is merely academic. The fact is that Bill Wylie is dead.

We were having a nice life. We had been married for twenty years, had four children: two girls, Liz and Kate, eighteen and seventeen, and two boys, John and Matthew, fourteen and twelve. Both of us were born in Winnipeg and had moved to Stratford five years earlier when Bill became general manager of the Stratford Festival Theatre. We had a split-level house with a swimming pool in the back yard, a Bassett hound, a cat, a tank full of tropical fish, friends and fun and a future. A nice life.

It changed in a twinkling, as they say, when I turned around and saw his head on the coffee table. He was dead then, though I didn't know it. I gave him mouth-to-mouth resuscitation, but asked my daughter to take over because I thought I must be doing it wrong. There was no response. It was too late. No second chances.

There is a kind of glory in sudden death: to go down at the peak of one's powers with both achievement and potential untarnished, all flags flying. The light is snapped off before it has had a chance to dim or fade. One giant step into the next world. But O pity the survivors! Mid-stride dying is very hard on them. They are left to face the overdue library books, the bouncing cheques (party deceased, funds frozen), the work-in-progress, the plans underway, the gifts on order, all the machinery of daily life that was in full production and that has suddenly stopped. No time to slow down, to re-tool, to lay off. No time to prepare.

There is an Anglican prayer that reads in part, "Preserve us from sudden death." It's a point well taken. Because sudden death does throw a terrible rock into the machinery of normal family living.

No more so, really, than the terrible agony of a terminal illness. That's the way my father went, with cancer, so I've had the dubious privilege of seeing it both ways. It is painful to watch helplessly while someone you love slips away from you. I watched my mother be the eyes and ears and hands of the world her husband was leaving, caring for him with a zeal that almost put her to bed, too. Swift, or agonizingly slow, when death strikes a family, life will never be the same.

Mercifully, one does not immediately realize that fact, however death arrives. First things first. And the first thing on the agenda is a funeral. Funerals are primitive. I always thought so and nothing has changed my mind. And yet, as one friend pointed out, they fulfil the necessary function of convincing everyone that the worst has really happened; he really is dead. And it gives the peripheral friends a chance to do their duty, nevermore to be seen. It's called "paying their respects," and I suppose that fulfils a need as well. Tradition and custom can carry one through an awful lot of swampy territory.

One of the dangers for the widow, though, is that it is done all too swiftly. Speed is not necessarily a good thing. Well-meaning friends are anxious to get everything done, arranged, finished, so that you can start getting over it. You don't ever get over it. Loss is permanent. Part of you has died, too. So a little wallowing at this time doesn't hurt, if people would only allow it. But our society seems to demand that we behave ourselves at funerals, and after. And we do. Deportment is all. Breakdowns are bad form. But a little howling at the moon might save a lot of tension later on.

One week after my husband's death I was alone with my children. It takes about the same length of time to be left alone with a new baby to bring up. In the latter case, nerves are offset by joy and anticipation. In the silence following the frenzied activity of funeral arrangements and people dropping in, the sad fact begins to sink in: life will never be the same again. You are definitely alone. With a lot to learn. As one friend put it: it took me twenty years to learn to live with my husband; I wasn't going to unlearn overnight. Neither will you.

Mourning is a natural and necessary process. It shouldn't be rushed. For in grieving over the loss of another, what we are really doing is grieving over our loss of self, all the self that was invested in that person. We have to get it back somehow.

Freud said that the bereaved has to withdraw her emotional attachment from the deceased. "Withdraw the libido," he said, and, at the same time, begin to "internalize the lost love object." That means letting go, letting go of your husband, without losing your memories of him. You have to build a new relationship with him, and you have to become a new you. It takes time. It can't be hurried.

Grief is an illness with recognizable symptoms. Loss of sleep and loss of appetite contribute effectively to a general exhaustion. There may be headaches, stomach aches, bowel upsets, perhaps even a rash as a result of tension. A dreadful apathy can overtake you, and a withdrawal from reality. Sometimes you can see, more often hear, your husband in another room. For weeks after Bill died I could hear the evening paper rustling as he turned the pages. You lose contact with reality; you lose your trust in life. Death seems much simpler than life and much more welcome. One widow wrote, "I remember I used to think each night as I said my prayers that I was one day nearer the end of my life – and glad of it. That feeling left me."

Note that. The feeling left her. It does, you know. Bereavement is a terrible mental wound, slow to heal, but it does heal. It just takes time. Terrible cliché and not quite true. It also takes hard work. It isn't going to go away all by itself. You have to work at it.

Life, as my oldest daughter said to me, suddenly becomes an uncharted adventure. I found that hard to understand when she said it. I resented it and pushed it away from me. I had been content with my life as it had been, known and charted and secure and happy as it was. Why should I be comforted by the promise of unknown hazards and adventures? And yet, four years later, I see what she meant. How did she know so much?

In his strange and wonderful book *Living Your Dying*, Stanley Keleman hints at the same idea. "Endings," he writes, "bring us face to face with the unknown. Endings force us to make new relationships, or at least offer that opportunity. . . . Many people will say 'that person is irreplaceable to me.' The truth of the matter is that making an ending forces us to start being more self-reliant, or at least offers that opportunity."

No one ever told you it was an opportunity before.

2

From grief to joy

Joy does not mean riotous glee but it does
mean the purposive employment of energy in a
self-chosen enterprise. It does mean pride and
self-confidence. It does mean communication
and co-operation with others, based on delight
in their company and your own . . . to have
something to desire, to make, to achieve, and
at last something genuine to give."

Germaine Greer

In a death-denying society like ours, the crisis of bereavement is a tough one to face, because no one wants to let you face it, and no one wants to share it either.

"Cheer up," people say. "You have your children." Or your memories, or your health, or your money. But your husband is gone.

"Pull yourself together," they say. "There are worse things than death." They're right, of course, but name one.

16

"Stiff upper lip," they say. "He wouldn't want to see you like this." What's so bad about a quivering lower one? I'd like there to be a little breast-beating when I go, just to let me know I was missed.

"Carry on," they say. "You have to get up and keep going." Why?

In all other cases of shock, we are told the recommended treatment is rest and warmth. Pile on the blankets and the comfort. Why should it be any different for the shock of death? An electric blanket may be a poor substitute for a husband, but at a time like this it's the closest thing to the womb there is – a place to retreat to and lick one's wounds.

Psychologists have only recently recognized the deep needs of the survivor, and the patterns that grief must take if one is to recover and go on living a meaningful life. The whole process is described as "grief work," and it is very hard work. No part of it can be shirked. If it is, it will have to be faced and gone through at a later date, often with severe complications. After the initial, blessed numbness has worn off, there are hostility and guilt and depression to be worked through before any acceptance can be achieved.

Roughly classified, the stages of grief may be described as shock, denial, and acceptance, but a more detailed analysis may prove to be of some value. You'll find a number of variations depending on whose book you read, but here is a fairly comprehensive list:

I Shock
    1. Initial shock
    2. Emotional release
    3. Loneliness

II Denial
    1. Depression
    2. Panic
    3. Hostility

4. Guilt
5. Inability to return to normal activity

III Acceptance
1. Gradual hope
2. Struggle to affirm reality

The whole process can take well over a year, and there is always the chance after that of an unpredictable relapse when some unexpected, heartbreakingly simple commonplace suddenly reduces you to helpless tears. Bear with it. These symptoms do not necessarily follow the order of my neat column, nor does everyone suffer all of them. But they may serve as a guide to the kinds of emotions a widow must work through to earn her wings (not angel wings – wings of hope). The comfort in confronting such a list is the realization that you are not alone. Others have gone this path before you as there will be others after you. I know. I've been that way myself.

The psychiatrist Dr. Thomas Holmes has listed those life events that cause stress in human beings, with a stress-rating for each event. The event with the highest number of stress points is the death of a spouse with a box score of 100; next on the list is divorce with a score of 75. Holmes's idea is that no one should accumulate a life stress score of more than 200 in any given twelve-month period. A higher score can lead to serious illness, injury, or accidents. This is why one of the best pieces of advice a recent widow can listen to is: "Don't do anything rash."

Even if she doesn't do anything, there are changes that accompany the loss of her husband which automatically add to her stress. A change in financial status carries a score of 38; her finances have automatically undergone a change, and she won't be certain how she's fixed for a few months. Change to a different line of work is worth 36 points, or a business readjustment is 39. Within the year, if she wasn't working before, it's likely she will start now. If she was working, there are still subtle differences: she is the sole breadwinner now and it changes the job as well as the person doing it. A change in work responsibility is worth 29. Changes in eating (15) and sleeping habits (16) also account for stress points, and these changes are impossible to avoid.

One widow assured me it would be six months before I would be able to taste food or sleep through the night. Another one, older, said it would be a year. I wouldn't say my sleeping habits have ever recovered.

I was always the last one to bed. Bill was the one who locked the doors, put the milk order out and the cat in the basement, and turned out the lights around me until I said, "Hey, wait for me!" Now I try, I do try, to get to bed at a reasonable hour – and then I write in bed. But if something happens to hook me, like a book, or a list, or a new idea, it's game over. I'm up till 3 or 4 A.M. and sleep seems a waste of time.

A change in social life also causes stress (18 points), and it's more than that. As you get cut out of the social stream, resentment increases, and that brings a stress of its own. Special events, even happy ones, bring stress to everyone. Christmas carries a score of 12, and the first one A.D. must carry a little more than that. In these stressful times, it's not hard to pile up a sizable score even without a Super Event to send it soaring. Each family has its own events which will add to the strain. My first child left home to go off to university within that first year – that's 29 points. One divorcée asked me what was the score if your oldest unmarried daughter had an abortion. Holmes didn't cover that one. You can see that even if you don't do anything, you have enough stress to work through without going out of your way to find some more.

That's why I say for at least a year, sit tight. Work through your grief. Don't add moving or other major changes to the already drastic change in your life, if you can possibly help it.

You have a lot of emotions, reflexes, and habits tied up in one person, and they have to be released before you go on. Mary Vachon, mental health consultant with the Clarke Institute in Toronto, describes your task this way: "You have to get back a lot of the emotion you invested in the dead person." She also says that the 37 per cent widowed under the age of sixty-five are the worst problem area; that is, they represent a high-risk group. Research was carried out at the Clarke Institute which led to the formation in February, 1976, of a new social agency, Community Contacts for the Widowed. Some of the facts the Clarke discovered illustrate the high-risk factor of widows in specific age brackets. For instance, in the year following the death of their husbands, the young widows studied experienced three times as many hospital admissions as other women of similar age. The widows studied experienced a 12 per cent increase in mortality during the first year of bereavement. And 32 per cent of widows suffer "marked deterioration in health" within thirteen months after their husbands' deaths compared to 2 per cent for the control group.

Mary Vachon listed the types of cases with the greatest risk factor:

1. those with poor social support;
2. those under forty-five whose husbands died suddenly; or, conversely, those over sixty-five, whose husbands suffered a lingering death;
3. those with an ambivalent relationship to the deceased (those who have the most difficulty recovering are those who had the worst marriages);
4. those who were denied the grief experience because of minimal funeral ceremonies;

5. those with previous psychiatric difficulties. (If they were suicidal before, their chances of death by suicide are greatly increased; suicide is a high risk for the first five years following a spouse's death.)

Like most widows I know, I behaved myself during the initial impact. I had an ulcer that did tend to stand at attention under stress, though, so my doctor deemed it advisable to give me a relaxant to keep my gut from taking me on an acid trip. It was mild, however, and used sparingly. I was fully aware of what I was doing and why. I have since heard of widows whose doctors thought they were doing them a favour by tranquillizing them out of their skulls during the first after-days of shock. I do not believe in such a practice, trying to turn a pill into a twentieth-century balm of Gilead. Nor do I believe in the indiscriminate use of sleeping pills. If you are fortunate enough to have a religious faith, you will find that prayer does much more than Nembutal.

One widow told me, "My electric blanket saved me." Me too. I used to turn it and the bedside lamp on long before bedtime, so that when I was finally ready to try to sleep, the light and warmth would welcome me. Sleep does return in time, though perhaps your sleep patterns will have changed. All your other patterns will have changed; why should sleep be different?

Use the time. Other widows besides me – and not necessarily writers – have used paper in the wee small hours of the night to keep them company and sane. With me it began with my sympathy letters – some 700 of them. I wrote long into the night, every night, for weeks and weeks, replying at length to each letter I had received. This, of course, kept me from facing that empty (but warm) bed.

I began to keep a diary every night. It was a substitute for my bedtime conversation with Bill. It also proved to be a wonderful release (note stage 2 in the list of recovery symptoms above). Emotional release comes in many different forms. Welcome them all, because you need them. Paper helps dry the tears. Tears will come, of course, and must not be denied. But sometimes, when the pain is too overwhelming, it helps to distance it a little, or at least set it slightly aside, by writing down what you feel.

I didn't always wait till bedtime. If something really got to me, I'd rush to my diary and write it all down. A lot of the early pages are tear-splattered, but ballpoint pens don't run. I think it's better to run to paper than to a tranquillizer. In my case it's almost as addictive, but there are fewer side effects.

I have since recommended a journal to a number of people, not necessarily widows, who were depressed. "Write it down," I say. "Get it on paper, and take a look at it." All who have tried it report that it helps. That's what those *Nothing Books* are for. Have you seen them? They are bound books of blank paper, no dates, nothing, just blank paper; much better than a page-a-day, dated diary with an imitation leather cover and a tinny lock and key – that's for teeny-boppers. If you can't afford the hardcover edition, there's a paperback *Nothing Book* on the market now. If, like me, you tend to write uphill and need lines, then get yourself a school scribbler. The important thing is to have a special notebook for your writing, and let it happen.

It's not only grief you may want to express. If you do get angry or resentful at people's treatment of you, at real or fancied slights, you can write it all down, let off all your steam, without saying anything you might be sorry for later. If, like me, you are a this-time-last-year kind of person, you can indulge in that to your heart's content, without boring anyone. Go ahead and dwell on your milestones. Recall – and write down – the happy times as well as the bad ones. Set yourself assignments. Thanksgiving is a good place to start. Each Thanksgiving I make a point of thinking of and writing down all the things I have to be thankful for. Work at it. Don't take anything for granted. Realize how blessed you are, and count your blessings by writing them down. Then, later, on a day when you've hit a low ebb, go back and read what you've written. That will help. You have just become your own therapist. Never underestimate the power of paper! Consider your diary your Withdrawal Book. And don't worry if you can't spell; no one's going to see it but you.

It's hard sometimes to distinguish between genuine grief and self-pity. "Our tears are selfish," wrote Peter Marshall in his book of sermons, *Mr. Jones, Meet the Master*, "for we are self-centred – self-absorbed. We keep thinking of what it means to us. We reflect how much we miss the departed, and we weep because we begrudge their going. We wish they had stayed on with us awhile. . . . We wish things had gone on as they were. We resent the change, somehow, never thinking what it must mean to them that are gone."

Self-pity is a kind of permissive self-dramatization. And grief is very like fear. "Perhaps," says C.S. Lewis, "more strictly, like suspense. Or like waiting; just hanging about waiting for something to happen. It gives life a permanently provisional feeling." Grief is an agonized apprehension of something that has already happened. It's standing at the edge of a void, a very recently carved hole that has forced a change in your direction. It is knowing, with a sinking feeling in your gut, that you have to go on, alone, and that's painful.

Pain takes many different forms. If you can let self-pity give way to irony, there's hope for you yet. One of my children gave me the best example to follow. John, at fourteen, went off to his beloved summer camp as planned. One night at camp a group of boys was sitting around a campfire talking, John told me later, and they began to compare notes on their fathers' occupations. "What does your Dad do?" John had no intention of telling them his father had died two months before; that would involve a singling-out he didn't want. When it came his turn to say what his father did, he said casually, "Well, he lies around a lot."

I remember my refusal of a gift of lilacs the first spring A.D. because my husband was allergic to them. It took me weeks to stop heading for the passenger side of the car, and over two years before I ever spread out in the double bed – there was a small neat dent where I carefully slept on my side, though I always turned on the blanket on his side, in case a stray leg got chilled in the night. The first roast I attempted to carve caused a few tears and some messy chunks of meat. Fortunately, roast beef is so expensive now we don't have the problem very often. It is not, in fact, for the predictably difficult situations that you must brace yourself, but for the simple events that can undo you. I was visiting friends and saw the wife slip a lipstick in her husband's pocket – all the preparation she needed to go out, since he had the money, identification, car and house keys. I used to do that too, and I can't any more. That hurt. But these are examples of self-pity – easy traps – and not to be tolerated.

The panic associated with the depression of loneliness (see list again) seems to come when you are expected to do something you have always let your husband do because he did it so much better. We women have all been pampered and protected into a state of near-incompetence. If feminism gives women a stronger sense of self, a larger competence in financial and mechanical matters, a greater confidence in their own abil-

24

ity to cope with life's practical problems, then it will ease the role of widows everywhere. The first time I had to back into a parking place in a car park I realized anew that I was alone. There was no one to do it for me; I had to do it myself. I did, of course. Out of that initial panic rose determination and, eventually, skill. Now I can squeeze back into spaces that you wouldn't believe.

And then you hit another aspect of the loneliness. When you do achieve something, you have no one to share it with. Your loving reflector is gone. As one widower put it to me, "I know well the temptations of self-pity and the danger of enjoying sympathy. These come, I think, because that special understanding, so generously given and so esteeming, has abruptly gone, and there remains a struggle not to shrink and become less of a person. Widow and widower are so terribly vulnerable."

Depression is a form of anger. The loss of a loved one generates a lot of hostility which must be worked through. Often the hostility is directed at the person who died. The widow feels she has been unfairly abandoned, and it's all his fault. All the if-onlies are his fault. I know one widow who told me that every time she hit a crisis during the first year following her husband's death she'd address him aloud: "John Smith," she'd shout, "why did you leave me to face this alone?"

If the marriage was less than ideal, a terrible guilt accompanies the anger. The survivor feels guilty that she wasn't nicer, more patient, more forgiving, more loving. Whatever faults her spouse threw at her in their bad scenes, she hurls at herself with a cruel ferocity. Fine. Let it all happen. All those emotions have to be recovered and worked out.

It was nearly forty years ago that psychiatrist Karen Horney concluded that we cannot deal with our anger unless we allow it to enter our consciousness. You have to recognize it and you mustn't be afraid of it. Maturity isn't denying anger, it's facing it. Repressing anger is dangerous, as is repressing grief. You have been deeply wounded, and you must act before gangrene sets in.

Anger is caused by some frustration – in this case, your husband's death – which has thwarted your hopes and plans for a future that included him in it. If you're not angry at him, then you turn your anger on others for frustrating you: for ignoring you, you think; for forgetting you; for not making a fuss over you; for excluding you; in short, for going on living their own lives.

To rid yourself of anger you must either remove the obstacles in the path of your frustration or recognize what these obstacles are and change your expectations. Well, you can't remove the death. But you can recognize the gap between your expectations and people's performance, and do one or several things about that.

1. Close the gap. Be more realistic in your expectations. Realistic, not cynical.
2. In the case of genuine slights, rebuffs, or disappointments, shrug your shoulders and give up. Write them off. It happens. "I've lost the Soanso's," I moaned to a friend. "No," my friend said, "they've lost you."
3. Concentrate on the goodies. Play the Glad Game. Marvel at the unlooked-for, unexpected kindnesses people have done you. Say it out loud. Write it down. Count your blessings. Keep counting.
4. When you cannot remove the cause of your anger, when it's permanent, as in this case, then find extra energy in yourself to cope with it. Direct that energy into a creative, satisfying outlet: a sport, a hobby, a volunteer job, a new project at work. Make your anger-energy work for you!

Some people get angry at God. But as one widow told me, "I think He's big enough to handle it."

In my case, I felt neither hostility nor guilt. My husband died such a sudden, freakish death that I could hardly blame him for leaving. He must have been as astonished as I was. And our marriage was so satisfying that it left nothing unsaid or undone. I'd have liked years more of it, mind you, but it was complete. Sometimes I now think, maybe we had it all, and that's why it ended. Who knows? But my depression did turn into anger. I was angry at most of my friends. I demanded more of them than anyone could possibly deliver, and since people don't deliver much to widows, there was quite a gap between their delivery and my expectations. If only we could tell people the kind of help we need and expect.

At first we need someone to talk to, to pour it all out at, to go over the details of our life and his death until we have it all together and begin to accept it as reality and not some nightmare we may eventually waken from.

Next, we need someone to count on, some semblance of routine. Activity really does help, and widows left with children at home are fortunate in the sense that they have people they must do something for. A friend can, however, offer a regular visit or a planned activity to look forward to and count on for a few weeks or months.

A friend can also help with that next phase in our little list: inability to return to normal activity. It was a good friend who made me return to our weekly swimming class at the Y, and who made me have our annual swimming party at the end of the season. It was my own common sense that made me return to the church choir sooner than anyone else recommended.

When death has reduced "normal" to a meaningless

27

word, any semblance of normal routine is a great help. Anything that gives you some kind of focus can help to keep you sane in those first terrible months of re-adjustment. That's why work can be a blessing. Gradually, unbidden, stray streamers of hope lighten the darkness. You know now it's not a case of getting over, it's getting through it.

Happiness is not a pursuit in itself and does not come on command. Happiness is a by-product which sneaks up on you, unsought, when you're busy at something else. Joy, on the other hand, is a positive activity, one that is every person's duty to cultivate. I believe you must work at joy. Demand it as your right; pursue it as your goal; give it to others as your obligation to them.

One of the first things you can do, as you look around in your increasing light, is find someone else who needs help. One widow wrote me: "A source of strength is either to phone or go to see someone who is in far worse straits – and one does not have to look far." There are self-help programs operating here and there across the country, widows helping widows, and that's not a bad place to begin.

Only widows, or, if one is lucky, one's closest friends, can know what another widow is going through. It's a sisterhood with terrible dues, a membership you would avoid if you could. Once arrived, however, your capacity for compassion and sympathy and practical help expands enormously. Heart and hands reach out to help others in pain and need. And this, perhaps, is the greatest affirmation of reality a person can achieve.

3

Changing your lifestyle

*The most difficult adjustment a woman is
called on to make is learning to live alone after
being married.*

Isabella Taves

A widow is not immediately aware of how different her
life is. At first the changes seem minute. You go on in
the house. You stick to the routine, especially if you
have children. You do what must be done each day –
cleaning, cooking, shopping. Familiar tasks are a blessing and a comfort. It's almost as if your husband were
away on an extended business trip. Almost. There is less
laundry, of course. The pressure of producing a great
dinner every night, if you ever felt such a pressure, eas-
es. Your social life drops like a stone.

The first thing you notice is that you have a lot more
time on your hands. There is no one to coax you to have
another cup of coffee, a drink, a chat, a walk. You seem
to have become more efficient, but time hangs heavy.
What do you want to save it for?

Little by little, though, the changes become more apparent and more drastic. It's as if the two of you had been arrows shot from two bows, your paths parallel. The event that stopped the flight of one arrow has deflected the path of yours. Little by little, the trajectory will be greatly changed. You're flying on alone. What happens, ultimately, is that your whole lifestyle changes.

This is a secret that your friends and acquaintances know before you do: you are a different person. External circumstances are going to force changes in you that you never expected. It's irrelevant whether or not you wanted them; they're going to happen. Life has written you a new script.

Since your future has changed so much, you might as well get ready for it by taking a long hard look at your life right now. Everything you have been accustomed to doing bears scrutiny and re-evaluation. Start by questioning your daily routine. Why are you doing what you do in the way that you do it? Habit? Or necessity? For whom are you running your household now? What are your priorities?

You were probably running the house for your husband before. Dinner was set in accordance with the time he came home. Your shopping and free time were arranged to accommodate your social life together. If you worked as well, then you had, no doubt, reciprocal arrangements and divisions of labour, but it was team work. Everything you did was done with someone else's needs in mind. Marriage, we are told, is supposed to be an equal partnership, but some partnerships are more equal than others. And in most cases the older the widow, the more male-dominated the household was. Most marriages in this century and on this continent have acknowledged the male as the head of the household. Life With Father is a twentieth-century truism.

Now that Father isn't there, it's time you took a good look at yourself. Otherwise you're going to atrophy like

Queen Victoria. Everyone knows the story of her devoted grief, how the room was kept as it always was, and Albert's clothes laid out every day. No one expects or admires that kind of paralysis on the part of a widow today.

Speaking of clothes, you should remove your husband's clothes from the house as soon as possible. It is more important that he take a permanent place in your heart and memory than be revered in a moth-eaten sweater. I gave shirts to nephews, underwear and socks and pyjamas to the Salvation Army, and sold the good suits to a second-hand clothing store. The beautiful ties, which my husband collected and prized, I gave away to his closest men friends, to remember him by, at least as long as they were in style. Empty the closet and open your heart.

And stay open. You're going to have to keep an open mind if you're going to change, and you have to change, though slowly at first. Little by little you realize you don't have to cater to other people's needs all the time; in fact, it's time you started paying some attention to your own. You're the only one who's going to.

And that's the next step to total assessment. You begin to take a look at all your habits, and you start to analyze how you got that way, why you do this or that, and you begin to question the necessity of continuing in the same – not pattern – rut.

The first changes are the hardest and the most exciting – even simple ones like shifting shopping times or your laundry habits. Your cooking habits change, too, and not always for the better. The widow living alone has the biggest problem in the kitchen. I read recently that a single person pays at least 10 per cent more for food because of the inability to buy in quantity at lower prices. Even one tin of something lasts two or three meals, and boredom sets in, accompanied by a lack of appetite. My father, a doctor, used to say that women living alone subsisted on a diet of tea and toast and corn flakes – "No fit food," he used to say, "for growing females." The widow living alone should try to maintain good eating habits to ensure her health. If that sounds too preachy, I'm sorry. But you have a long time to go on alone; you might as well do it in good health.

One of the hidden bonuses of being single is that you are in control. You make the decisions now, so don't be afraid to experiment. Why not have soup for breakfast (I like cream soup best), or a gigantic baked potato loaded with butter or sour cream (but nothing else except maybe a salad) for dinner? Make a point, if you can afford it, of having a guest at least once a week, for lunch or dinner, or for coffee and dessert. It's not only good for your morale and your appetite, but if you choose your guest wisely, it will also result in a return invitation, which is even better for the morale and the appetite.

Cooking presents different problems to the working mother, to the scrimping housewidow, and to the lonely, older widow. Each situation, however, is sure to be different from what it was before. As a working mother you have to be sure your children are getting the best nutrition possible with the least amount of effort and maximum efficiency on your part. Obviously, you can't spend hours in the kitchen fussing about food. At the same time, you can't simply broil a fast chop every night. That's too expensive, and dull. There never has been a time when more information was available for whatever problem has to be handled. The libraries and bookstores are crammed with cookbooks, and there are a lot of them dedicated to casseroles, do-ahead foods, the specific problems of a working cook, or cooking for one or two. Similarly, if money is a problem – and when isn't it? – there are cookbooks that tell you how to get the most nutrition, fun, and good taste for your food dollars.

Surveys have indicated that women without men do not set as good a table as they did. The image you had of yourself as Earth Mother, Hostess Bountiful, Giver of All Good Things to Eat, seems to have disappeared. The reasons are understandable enough. You don't have the same incentive that you did. You've lost your most appreciative audience. You don't have as much money. Lots of reasons. Old Mother Hubbard's cupboard was bare – it's obvious she was a widow.

This change is almost imperceptible as it happens; it creeps up on you by degrees. As a matter of fact, until I moved, I kept on running a household for six, even though two and then three of the occupants were no longer with us. My oldest daughter went off to university the fall after my husband died, followed by my second daughter the year after. I had three fridges and a freezer, and I seemed to keep on filling them, though I must admit I had more trouble emptying them than before. It wasn't until I was in a three-bedroom apartment with one refrigerator that I began buying and cooking for three instead of six, and that's when I found I couldn't always have an extra one or two for dinner on short notice. Of course, that wasn't the only reason. My typewriter, by that time, was far more important to me than my kitchen. You see, changes sneak up on you, whether you are aware of them or not.

The way you spend your time changes more than the way you set your table. The absence of your husband changes the way you spend almost every moment of your life, especially the moments you used to spend together. Times when you are most empty and unoccupied, like the hour before dinner when he used to come home and talk over the day, or Saturday night which you used to spend together – these are the very times when your married friends are busiest with their husbands. You must fill that time for yourself.

The dinner hour is the easiest to fill. You simply move it forward; you don't have to wait for anyone to come home, and kids are always happy to eat early. It gives you a longer evening, but you'll learn to fill that productively, and even be grateful for the time. If you're working, there's less problem with empty times on weekdays. You'll be too busy to notice when you have to do everything yourself.

I know a lot of widows who write letters, pay their bills, and balance their budgets on Saturday nights. Other nights it is possible to find single things to do – meetings to go to, activities to occupy yourself – but Saturday seems to be couple-oriented, like the society we live in. If you want to be occupied on Saturday night, you're going to have to plan ahead. As a matter of fact, all singles have to do a great deal of planning ahead. You don't have a built-in companion for whatever spontaneous activity comes to mind.

I have on occasion gone out to dinner on a Saturday night with a wrench of widows, but I don't recommend this as common practice. Tickets for many events are more expensive on Saturdays, and restaurants are usually more crowded. It doesn't matter that there are five or six of you, if you're all female, the waiter says, "Oh, you're alone," and puts you near the kitchen door. Get a TV Guide or buy some pretty stationery and a new address book and brush up on your correspondence instead.

Sunday is white-knuckle day. It helps to go to church, if you are that way inclined (I am). Some working mothers find it helps to sleep in. If you're a working mother you may be doing the laundry and other household chores on Sunday afternoon. This is often more productive and less depressing than a walk. Walking is best with two.

For a while I tried to fill Sundays by having guests for dinner, either whole families that my children would enjoy, or singles that they could help to entertain. It gave us all a focus, I thought, to concentrate on someone outside ourselves on Sunday afternoon. It helps – for a while. If you have been accustomed to cooking a good Sunday dinner, you won't feel the pressure of having "company" as much. If you look around, you can find any number of waifs and strays who would enjoy a Sunday dinner. There are lots of singles around who are as lonely as you are. In fact, singles are better than families. You don't expect them to reciprocate.

After one season I quit having people for Sunday dinner. No one ever asked us back – that's how it gradually dawned on me that my friends had changed. Don't dwell on it when it happens to you. Accept what has happened and move on. Anyway, company for Sunday dinner became less and less attractive because (a) it's expensive, and (b) it's tiring. There are some weeks you just don't have the time or energy to make a special dessert.

You will find, as time goes by, that the people you have over and the people who invite you to their homes differ from the people you used to see when you were part of a couple. That's the way it goes. You are a different person now, and you're not the only one who has learned how different you are. One plus one equalled a couple before, and you and your husband moved easily among a group of friends who considered you a unit. Like Mutt and Jeff. Ham and eggs. But in the eyes of the world, or at least of the society you live in, two take away one doesn't equal one. Most of the time it equals nothing. Face it: you are odd woman out. Very few people want seven or nine or eleven, let alone thirteen, at their dinner tables. Most people think you'd rather not come alone to their parties. They think tickets come in even numbers.

The remarkable thing is that other people change faster than you do. You still cling to the idea that you are a person, a human being in your own right. No one else does. You are going to have to change their minds for them, and in the process you will undergo a few changes yourself.

Never mind. If you're forgotten when it comes to playtime, you're Number One on the list when it comes to work – unpaid, of course. I mean, you have all that time on your hands. The first fall after my husband's death I was not invited out to dinner but I was asked to run a publicity campaign for the local Y, bake pies for the church bake sale, sell books for the Y book sale, canvass for the United Appeal, be an area manager for a fund-raising drive, and fill in on short notice as a fourth at bridge. I hate bridge.

Maybe what people do to you actually helps while it hurts. It hurts at the time but you begin to learn the hard way that you really are alone. As my first Christmas A.D. approached, one of my closest friends said to me, "I'd invite you all for dinner on Christmas but you have to face reality sooner or later." I thought I had been facing reality for six months, daily. Suttee, the practice whereby the widow throws herself on her husband's funeral pyre, has been outlawed in India. They still practise a subtle form of it in Canada. You die by inches, of loneliness.

If you think I'm being too bitter or grim or harsh, bear with me. I'm stating the facts first, in their plainest terms. There are, of course, wonderful exceptions, sources of help and comfort you never expected – and often not from the friends you have relied on over the years. A drastic change has occurred in your life, and it sets off a chain reaction of changes all the way down the line, in friends and family and society, as well as in your whole lifestyle.

Well, that's as bad as it gets. From here on in, you

have nowhere to go but up. It's a long climb but you have lots of time, and you have an asset no one, maybe even you, realizes. Yourself. If you weren't before, you are about to become your own best friend.

Having told you the worst, let me now reassure you. There never has been a time in history when it has been more exciting to be a single woman. The feminist movement is only a few years old, but it has already loosened some of the codes and paved the way for a single woman to make a new life for herself as a vital, functioning, contributing person. It is still up to you, of course, but others have stuck their feet in doors for you. The future is yours in a way that it never has been before. Whether you find that challenging or frightening depends on you.

If friends invite you somewhere – anywhere! – say yes. Don't give them the excuse not to ask you next time because "you'd only say no anyway." They find their own reasons quickly enough. If you're working and there's an office party, go to it. You may end up on sandwich detail or the punch bowl, but go. If you're invited to a wedding and you have no one to go with, go anyway – and that goes for cocktail and any other kinds of parties, dinners, theatre performances, home-and-school or annual meetings, political rallies, anything. Go! You will find you have to draw some lines at volunteer work because the invitations in this area are endless. You need to decide where you will devote your energy and time and where your saturation point is, because it's in you, not in the work to be done.

One of the things I didn't know I knew, I learned from my widowed mother and aunts whom I had unconsciously observed before I became a widow myself. I watched these widows say no and dwindle. Mind you, they were a lot older than I was, and it was harder for them to say yes. Saying yes means making an effort, spending some energy, and maybe even some money, and taking risks. So my motto as a widow is: "Never say no to anything – within reason!" I have ended up in some peculiar situations because of this, and I have had some rotten times. But I have also had some unexpectedly good times and met a few really enjoyable people I might not otherwise have met. As a newly single person, you have to keep meeting new people, you see, because a lot of your old relationships are no longer valid. You are the one who's changing, though it seems at first that other people have.

Some friends may forget you at the dinner table, but I have found that a single woman is far more welcome as a house guest than a couple. A single woman can fit in the spare room, help with the kids, pitch in with the cooking, and adapt to any plans going on in a busy, active household far more readily than a couple.

Travel is a wonderful form of escape. Every widow I know will go anywhere at the drop of a hat or a ticket. I have never refused any trip or visit that is offered me and I have been the grateful recipient of food, drink, hospitality, and even airline tickets from dear, kind, generous friends.

I still feel alien on this planet without my husband. Somehow, when I am away from home, I feel less strange, in a perverse sort of way. I mean, I'd be foreign anyway. And I like the feeling of being suspended in space and time, of having, for the time being, no real responsibilities, no commitments, no pressures. So often, since Bill died, I have asked myself in wonder, "What am I doing here?" When I'm on a trip I know the answer. I'm visiting.

So I have travelled a lot since his death and rarely stay in hotel rooms. I have learned how to be a guest, and I have become closer friends with my long-distance friends and their children than I might ever have had the opportunity to be otherwise.

I like flying alone. I like driving alone. But I find that I cannot get used to going to movies or the theatre alone. Everyone has his threshold of intolerance and this seems to be mine. I have done it, but I don't like it. I have sought a few friends, those with busy husbands or none at all, who like movies as much as I do, and I go with them. Or else I go with my boys, which limits the choice of movie these days. I am more aggressive about the theatre. I get myself a single ticket and offer dinner before or drinks and supper after to a couple I know is also going. Or I get two or three tickets and offer myself as a package deal. This usually results in dinner on the man or the couple. The point is that anything is possible; you just have to plan a little more. One single complained to me that life had become once again one long series of dates.

It's true. You have to plan ahead. It takes money and time and energy to maintain a social life, and all three have decreased for the widow. It's a whole new ballgame, and it requires a whole new set of ground rules. You start by trying to fill in lonely gaps – the dinner hour, Saturday nights, Sundays. You progress to theatre-going, travel, new interests, maybe even, in time, new men. But we'll get to that later.

Brace yourself. You have to develop a single psyche again. As one friend said to me, "Just remember you're not married any more." It's painful, but it bears repeating, because after all these years of marriage, it's hard to remember.

As you go on, you see, the changes get both easier and more drastic. You change your emphasis. You realize that people are more important than things, that your children are more important than your routine, that you are more important than conventional habits.

Habit is a comfortable skin that cushions a lot of shocks. Shedding the skin can be painful. Change is always painful. But you have had the biggest change of your life thrust upon you. No choice. If you don't change to meet it, you won't survive.

4

Coping with money

Money may not be important but it quiets the nerves.

Joe E. Lewis

Before my husband died my two chief problems in life were (1) how to find more time to write, and (2) how to lose weight. Now they are much more basic: sex and money. I don't know whether that represents progress or not.

"Sex," according to a contemporary greeting card, "is like money. When you don't have it, it's hard to think of anything else." Widows think about both a lot. This chapter is about money.

It's called instant cut-off when a death occurs. Banks know before your distant relatives that your husband has died, and the cheques and bills come trailing back along with the first sympathy cards: "Party deceased; funds frozen." Unless you have a joint account (and even a joint one gets gelatinous and slow) or a separate bank account, that means *your* funds are frozen, too. Even though you may not feel like eating, you and your family have to be fed. Even if you are alone, expenses go on and must be met. And all the ongoing machinery of life must continue to be oiled with money even while the wrench that has been thrown into it is being coped with.

What do you do after the bomb has fallen but before the smoke has cleared? Well, did you know that you can get an instant cash advance on your husband's life insurance policy? It is not generally known (I didn't know it), but you can often get a portion of the policy within two or three days as an advance on the policy settlement. Thus, there is instant money available to settle hospital and doctor's bills, pay funeral expenses, and clean up the outstanding bills remaining from a life in progress. Use your life insurance company. Not many people do, not enough. Surveys have shown that life insurance agents rank farther down on a list of widows' helpers than they should. Family, friends, and lawyers are above clergymen these days, but life insurance agents are low down on the list along with bankers and union representatives.

We had moved out of the city where our life insurance agent lived but he happened to be in our area at the time of my husband's death so he came to see me and meet my lawyer. He outlined what was available. His only advice to me was not to blow the money on a mink coat or a trip to Florida, and then he went away and I never heard from him again. His office sent my husband a birthday card two weeks later. I sent it back. But I have learned something since then and I'm telling you now. Yelp a little. Ask for help. Sound off. You are not a little lone widow, dependent on your meekness and other people's good will for casual handouts. You are a single human being with all the rights thereto appertaining, and you'd be amazed how many rights you have.

So – holler for help. And one of the first places you

should holler at is your life insurance company. I was assured, in the course of my research, that a widow can approach a life insurance company on her own, without a lawyer to hold her hand or guide her or speak for her.

"By all means," I was told, "get a lawyer and make your will – every widow should have a will – but when it comes to settling life insurance, you don't need a lawyer. You can do it all through your agent or the claims department."

A great deal that I wasn't even aware of was done for me by my lawyer. I wasn't aware of very much at the time. Perhaps it was a crippling kindness but who would question it? Mind you, I paid for it. *Chatelaine* magazine has a collection of Cope-Kits (available for fifty cents from *Chatelaine*, 481 University Avenue, Toronto). One is on how to settle an estate yourself – "and save $500, $1,000 and up" – by Constance Mungal. "Lawyers charge two per cent of the estate and take at least four months," the cover states. Right on.

I am not criticizing what was done for me. It had to be done because I was helpless. I had never even handled household accounts before Bill died, and now I was busy learning *everything*. And to think I had thought I was a reasonably liberated woman! It is shameful that I should have been so incompetent. If the feminist movement does nothing else, perhaps it will raise women's consciousness to a level of simple competence. Mine wasn't.

After the smoke has cleared and the bills are paid, you have to take stock of your financial position and start making some plans for the future. Learn something else I didn't know, and save yourself some money. All ordinary life insurance policies have settlement options, with a minimum guarantee period. In the zeal to get me settled and finished with, I was advised to cash in everything at once and re-invest the money to establish my basic widow's income. The result was I was hit with a whopping tax bill on the various pension and retirement monies that I took as a lump sum in one year. I learned later that it is possible to take this kind of money in regular payments spread over a period of time, thus reducing the tax in any given year. It depends, however, on interest rates. The insurance company doling out the payments to you is making interest on the capital. If you were to invest that capital for yourself, perhaps the income would compensate for your initial tax on its receipt. Or you might consider living on your capital, if you can, and rolling your husband's Registered Retirement Savings Plan and pension incomes into your own RRSP, thus bypassing the immediate tax on them. Nothing is simple, is it? Get some good professional help, ask a few questions, and find out what's best for you.

Virtually all group life insurance policies and many individual insurance policies and many individual policies have a disability waiver on them. If your husband had a prolonged terminal illness during which he was unable to work, it is possible that this clause on the policy will make premium payments unnecessary for the period of time he was disabled. If you were aware of it during the illness, it made for one less bill to pay. If you are not aware of it even now, ask. You may be entitled to a refund. Don't be afraid to ask. It might save you money, maybe even get you some back.

My father had arranged to buy a set of encyclopaedia a few months before his terminal illness was diagnosed. My husband and I said we'd take over the payments and the books because we had always wanted a set. A few months after my father's death I was going through some papers and found his contract with the book company. There was a clause that wiped out the payments in the event of the purchaser's death. I wrote the company and asked about this. They not only

43

cleared the remaining payments, they reimbursed us for the payments we had made since my father's death. You see, it doesn't hurt to ask.

Widows are often not aware of the group insurance their husbands may have through their work. Today about half of all life insurance policies are group insurance, and over 90 per cent of all employed people have group life insurance, so you should find out. Ask. Contact your husband's employer. Be sure to have your husband's social insurance number and his group insurance certificate number handy. See if you can find the booklet describing the group benefits; it will have instructions on how to make the claim. Incidentally, a disability premium waiver is universal on group insurance, so ask about the refund here, too. And while you're at it, ask about the pension fund, any accrued vacation or sick pay, terminal pay allowances, service recognition awards, unpaid commissions, credit union balance, whatever. Keep asking questions.

Frequently a long terminal illness can eat up all the insurance and savings, and a widow faces financial as well as emotional disaster. In cases where there is severe debt, a financial planner must be called in to help solve the problem. Talk to your bank manager. Talk to a lawyer, relatives, business friends. Ask questions. Ask for help. People often want to help but don't know how. Show them. Ask them. The world seems very harsh and empty right now, but there are hands out there waiting to help you. Reach out to them.

Which brings us up to right now. The moment of truth. How much is there to live on?

If you have been one of the fortunate competent women who handled your family's financial affairs, then you already know what it costs to run your household – correction: past tense – what it *did* cost. It is a sad and ironic fact that it will not cost as much. Husbands, bless them, are expensive. You not only have less food to prepare and less laundry to do, you also have less entertainment to pay for, fewer impulse purchases, and less drive to accumulate things. Yours is no longer an expanding economy, it is a shrinking one – an ironic blessing.

Anyway, perhaps you already have a budget, and know where the money goes. If not, sit down with one. Figure out what you need to live on now. Not everyone gets a chance to make a new life plan and a new budget. It's like three or four New Years rolled into one, and it may take a few resolutions. You can start fresh and try to build a perfect budget. Don't be surprised, though, when you fall short of perfection.

There are three basic financial rules. Even upgrading them to allow for inflation, they still apply to everyone. Ready?

1. Figure your net income, that is, after income tax and deductions. That's mostly what this chapter is about, figuring out your income. This is bottom-line time.

2. Figure on spending about half your income on shelter and food. The recommended percentages are 31 per cent for housing costs (that's *costs*, not just rent or mortgage payments), and 23 per cent for all food including restaurants. A warning: the lower your income, the more likely you are to exceed the one-half rule. You'll have to economize somewhere else.

3. Savings. Here's the rough one. Find a way to save – and tell me the secret! I have nothing to fall back on myself, except my native wit and my rather well-cushioned rear end. But you should aim for an amount in savings equal to 10 per cent of your net income. When you have that, put the rest in more inaccessible non-risk investments such as

45

guaranteed investment certificates or corporate bonds. The secret of savings, according to Sylvia Porter, author of *Sylvia Porter's Money Book*, is to consider your savings an unavoidable expense and allow for it automatically. I'm not sure whether that's called discipline or forethought.

Now you can, if you're lucky, set up your income in accordance with your predicted outgo. Easier said than done. In these days of inflation, with the cost of living so uncomfortably high, few life insurance policies are going to provide all the income a widow needs. But there are government cushions, and it might be wise to take stock of them right away.

First, for the younger widow with children at home, there is the monthly Family Allowance cheque. For older widows there is the Old Age Security Pension. Then there is the Canada Pension Plan, which pays a taxable cash settlement as well as a monthly allowance to the widow, and, direct to her, an allowance for each dependent child under eighteen. It doesn't happen automatically, only by application. Children over eighteen and under twenty-five who are still going to school and not married must apply to receive an orphan's allowance paid direct to them on proof of their attendance at a recognized institution of learning. The widow's applications for the death benefit and the monthly allowance usually go in together. They take time to process, and there may be a delay of a few months before the payments begin, but they are retroactive so the first cheque is a welcome, large one. There are Canada Pension offices in every city in Canada. In smaller centres, the Canada Pension person may operate only one day or part of a day a week. You can find out from your local post office, where he or she usually hangs out, which day of the week you can find him or her there.

If you live in Quebec the ground rules are a little different, but you may be eligible to receive a benefit under the Quebec Pension Plan. As in the case of the Canada Pension Plan, no benefits are available unless they have been duly applied for with the correct forms and documents. Forms and instructions are to be found in the Caisses Populaires or from regional offices of the Quebec Pension Board. The widow of a worker qualifies for a widow's pension if the deceased contributed to the Plan for at least three years and the widow is thirty-five years of age or more at the death of her husband, or though under age thirty-five at his death, she has at least one dependent child or is disabled. A widow who is not eligible at the death of the contributor may become eligible when attaining age sixty-five or if she becomes disabled before that age.

When you go to make your application for the government Pension Plan benefit, you will need to take the following with you:

1. the death certificate (funeral directors usually supply the death certificate; ask for a minimum of ten copies),
2. your husband's birth certificate,
3. his social insurance card,
4. your marriage certificate,
5. your birth certificate,
6. your children's birth certificates,
7. your social insurance card,
8. your children's social insurance cards, if any,
9. your husband's last income tax return, with its statement of contributory salary and wages. (Don't throw away his tax returns for five years.)

It's like a scavenger hunt gathering up these documents. Once you have them together, it's a good idea to keep them in a safe place because you'd be amazed at how often you'll have to refer to them again, especially the social insurance card. When I moved, repeated post office forms to Ottawa failed to change the address on my widow's allowance cheque. I finally phoned the Canada Pension office where I am living now and was told they could do nothing without my husband's social insurance number. Then as each child reaches the age of eighteen, he or she will need the number to make his or her own application for direct aid.

Another thing I learned: If you re-marry you are no longer a widow and your widow's allowance is cut off. If, however, the marriage doesn't work out, you can have the allowance re-instated. I think that's incredibly realistic and fair of the government.

All these government cheques are a source of income which you must take into account as you figure out your needs. If you have pension income coming to you from your husband's job as well, you can arrange to have that paid out over a period of years. Up to $1,000 a year is non-taxable. Similarly with a Registered Retirement Savings Plan or an annuity: both are taxable and tax can be sizable if you take them all in one lump, so stop and think about it. Here's a dandy little rule I was told: if the money you are getting is taxable, ask what your options are. How are you going to learn anything if you don't ask questions? But ask someone who knows the answers. The Canadian Life Insurance Association has a toll-free hot line which exists to answer your questions about life insurance. The number is 1-800-261-8663 (from British Columbia 112-800-261-8663).

Ask yourself a lot of questions. How much do you need? How long will it last? How much basic income can you count on each month? What other potential sources of income are there? Are the children old enough to work, or will they be soon? Should you take a course to increase your earning power? If you are already working, will your income plus your other sources be enough to tide you over? Or if you are a younger widow with children still at home, will you have to take your settlements in fairly big lumps over a short period of time to tide you over?

Tide you over to what? Good question. Tide you over to the point where you can bring in extra income of your own or to the point where you need less income because your children have left home – or both.

If you decide you have to work to supplement your income, and most widows do, perhaps you need some job-training before you can qualify to enter the work force, or, if you already have a job, to increase your skills and hence your income. You may want to take your settlement in large monthly payments over a period of two (five? ten?) years until you are able to qualify and become a breadwinner yourself.

The first important thing is to establish your immediate needs. Talk them over with your life insurance agent and settle on the amount of money required. Even if it's not going to last very long at the rate you need it, at least it will give you time to plan. Spread the money out as far as it will go.

As your children leave the nest, expenses will decrease. In the meantime, there are lots of ways to economize. Everyone, according to a supermarket survey of buying habits, is buying more rice and pasta these days to supplement the meat. You can do that. Get a cookbook on Mexican or Italian or Chinese food from the library and start experimenting, if you haven't already, with more economical types of cooking. It's a North American myth that we need to eat all that expensive beef. We may be the last generation to believe it, too, because our grain-fed cattle are using grains the rest of the world's people could use to eat.

You can cut back on clothing, too, and social and

recreational activities automatically get cut off once you are a widow. In fact, you'll save so much money in that department you'll have to have a party once in a while for the sake of your morale.

Magazines and newspapers are full of budget and cost-cutting ideas. Here are a few gems I picked up:

1. If you get a raise or a gift of money or any unlooked-for, unexpected income, pretend you didn't. Don't spend it. Put it into your savings account.
2. Get rid of your loose change. I save my dimes and quarters now for the laundry machines in my apartment. Nickels and pennies go into Matt's piggy bank – a painless way for him to save some money.
3. Don't carry credit cards with you. Of if you feel you must, try leaving them at home one week a month. See if you don't spend less money. Money experts say people spend at least 10 per cent more when they buy by credit card. It's too easy.
4. If you have a bank loan or a system of payments on a car or furniture, don't stop making the payments after you've paid up. Just put the same amount regularly into your savings account. It's called discipline.
5. Don't carry as much cash as you did, if you did. See how little you can get along on. (But don't be chintzy.)
6. Shop for groceries right after a meal so that you're not hungry and reaching impulsively for food. Impulses in supermarkets can add 25 per cent to your grocery bill. Make a shopping list and stick to it.
7. That means making a menu plan for the week. A plan saves not only money but time.

8. Try saying no for a week. No chocolate bars, no magazines, no movies, no meeting a friend for lunch or coffee. You might even lose some weight, and I have met very few women who ever minded that.

If you have a car and you continue to drive it, you should let your car insurance agent know that your husband is dead, and make sure you are covered for driving. This caution does not apply to women who do not drive or who don't own a car. For those who don't drive it is a question of selling the car or giving it to one of the children. Or taking driving lessons. What I needed was geography lessons.

I had a different kind of decision to make. Just weeks before his death, my husband had ordered a new car, a big heavy one equipped with all the extras: stereo, 8-track tape, cruise control, etc. It was a floating living room, hardly the kind of vehicle a lorn widow lady needed. So one of the first things I had to do was to go down to the car dealer and make arrangements for a smaller, more modest car to suit my reduced needs.

If you're having trouble with your car, start asking more questions. There are places you can go to do your own car repair where you just pay for the parts, but I'm sure not many of us want to go that far. Even allowing for my liberated conscience, I also have to allow for my personal preference. I prefer to have someone do the work for me. I was very proud of myself the first time I filled the gas tank at a self-serve gas station – that's as far as I want to go with do-it-yourself car maintenance. If you feel the same way, find yourself a reputable car dealer or mechanic and stay with him. Ask around. People have favourites. You're bound to find someone who will make the car sing for you without charging the earth. Bear in mind that earth costs more these days. So does gasoline.

The price of gasoline is going to continue to rise, we are told. If you live in a city with good access to public transportation, you may find that you will save a lot of money by getting rid of the car entirely. On the other hand, suburbia and young children make a car more of a necessity. It has been proven several times by people with heads for figures that taking taxis can be cheaper than owning and driving a car in a city now, but it's inconvenient when it rains. Older widows I know, like my mother, take taxis, but a lot of them take other people too – out of their way. People drive widows and save them the taxi fares. You have to figure your options, and not only on insurance.

There is a grey area surrounding women and credit. As a widow you are more respectable than a divorcée in the eyes of the cliché-ridden public, and you can often coast on your husband's credit rating if you don't have one yourself. Lots of widows simply don't tell the various department stores and oil companies that their husbands are deceased and go on paying their bills. Few companies notice that Mr.'s signature no longer appears on the cheques. Some of the big ones don't care, it seems; widows I know who have gone to the trouble of informing them of change of name and status at the time of a move have simply had cards re-issued with the address changed and nothing more.

Until you have borrowed money in your own name and paid it back, you don't have a credit rating. Even if you don't need money right now, it might be a good idea to go through all the motions, get a bank loan and invest the money or put it into an RRSP. (In this case you can get an income tax deduction on the money you invested.) Assert yourself.

And you may have to. Although there are no discriminatory laws on Canadian books regarding women and credit, and although company and bank policies now are stated to be favourably inclined to dealing with women, there is still a gap between theory and practice. It takes a while for company policy to seep down into the ranks of the clerks and managers who will be dealing with you. Horror stories abound: about the working mother, a widow, sole support of her family, with a good income, who was required to get the signature of her sixteen-year-old son before she could get a department store credit card; about another single woman who had managed to keep her family and herself for years but who couldn't get a mortgage without her father's signature – and he was seventy-five and living on his Old Age Pension! My widowed mother was issued a Chargex card with Mr. on it. She sent it back explaining she was Mrs. They sent her a new card with her correct title but a lower credit rating. The S meant $ to the bank. My bank has no category for widow in its application form for a key account. A widowed friend of mine met confusion in the form she had to fill out when she wanted to open a high-interest, no-checking savings account at her bank. "If widowed or divorced," read the form, "give husband's name and address." Yes indeed.

That widow has this advice to give: Don't be timid. Bear down. If you're asking for a loan, walk in with a list of your assets, both fixed and liquid and "shove it at them." Don't try to reform the system. If they balk at you, say you'll go elsewhere or ask for a higher authority. If that sounds like assertiveness training, you're absolutely right.

If you get or already have credit cards, use them, by all means. But use them as if you were using cash. It's safer that way. I have found that it is better to operate on a cash basis. Widows and freelance writers (and I am both) have this in common: their futures are more precarious than most and their incomes are smaller, not to say variable. So I do not buy on time. I stay out of debt beyond my current monthly expenses. I would resent paying the over-18 per cent carrying charges if I merely paid my minimum monthly payment on a credit card. I can't afford that, and neither can you. Debt is a downward spiral that widows should stay out of.

One of the biggest debts I had was the mortgage on the house, but this was wiped out by a life insurance policy. There are policies for mortgage cancellation. Find out if you have one. Even if you do not have such a policy, it might be wise, if there is enough money, to pay off the mortgage and own your home clear. Little widow ladies tend to feel more secure if they are women of property, and real estate continues to be one of the best investments you can make.

Here is another little-known fact I was told. Normally mortgage companies want an interest bonus when the mortgage is paid off. But if a widow explains that she is using a life insurance policy to pay off the mortgage, the bonus may be waived. (Mine was.) The moral to the story is: it doesn't hurt to ask! Write a personal letter. Big institutions are human, too, often more human than an individual who holds only one or two mortgages and needs his income from the interest.

But while we're on the subject of your home, you will be deciding sooner or later whether or not you're going to stay there. Make it later. One of the most important things any widow can learn is to sit tight, and this applies to sex as well as to money. Make few quick decisions, at least, few basic ones. You will have enough to do getting your heart and head together. Don't do anything rash. Wait at least a year, if you possibly can, before you decide whether to move or to make any other major changes in your life. Your children will appreciate this too, if you still have children at home. Life will have changed enough for all of you without imposing other upheavals. So get your money settled, try to establish a living plan for the immediate future but *don't do anything drastic!*

The future stretches a long way ahead of us. Widows with younger children must pay attention to their needs and the more immediate future, but all of us have to prepare for a long, lonely road with whatever resources we have, and sometimes they are extremely limited.

You wonder as you grow older whether you will out-live your money. Good question, and I have no easy an-swer to that. Fixed incomes become less and less effec-tive as prices keep on rising with no end in sight. You simply have to try to salt something away for that twil-ight zone we are all approaching, while seeking the best returns for your money right now. "God will provide," goes the proverb, "and I wish He would till He does."

"From birth to eighteen," said Sophie Tucker, "a girl needs good parents. From eighteen to thirty-five she needs good looks. From thirty-five to fifty-five she needs a good personality. From fifty-five on, she needs good cash." In Canada the average age at which a woman is widowed is fifty-six, and what she needs is good cash. And no matter what the amount, you are the one who has to make the decisions about your widow's mite. It's your future you're talking about, and there ain't nobody else going to look after you.

There are some wives today who still scarcely know how to write a cheque. I could do that, but I couldn't balance a chequebook. I still can't because I can't add or subtract worth a damn. But I can stay within a budget and I pay my bills on time and I'm juggling a job and feeding my family and I feel stronger than I have ever felt.

It's not easy and it's not simple, but there are helps and guides and signposts along the way, and if you don't know where you're going, it doesn't hurt to ask. It's amazing how much information you can get if you ask a direct question!

5

Moving on

*How quickly, in one instant, years of happy
life become only memories!*

Pearl Buck

There is a phrase engineers use to describe the position
of an object when it stops moving. It is called the "angle
of repose." Your husband has reached his angle of repose but you haven't. You haven't stopped moving yet.
As long as we live we keep on changing.

The first autumn after Bill died, I went ahead as
usual and made jams, jellies, pickles, etc. I don't have a
second hand on my watch or my kitchen clock. I always
used to use my husband to time my jelly-stirring (or
count "a-thousand-and-one-"). So when I had to stir my
jelly that first fall, I ran upstairs and got his watch to
help me out. It was the first time I had looked at it. The
date had changed – it stopped 12 hours after he died.

I can stand that, I thought. I can stand that. And I
can. I can stand anything. I didn't know that before. You
can, too.

I haven't made jelly since, or pickles, but for other

56

reasons than you might suspect. First, my family did not use up the supplies within the year as they did before. Second, I lost my interest in cooking. Third, I became too busy doing other things. Fourth, there is no storage space in my new home for preserves. You see, I moved.

Divorce, quipped a recent divorcée, is learning how to change your own lightbulbs. That applies to widowhood, too. I know there are lots of married women who change the lightbulbs, and take out the garbage, too, but it is a comforting knowledge that there is another, usually taller, person in the house who can change a ceiling bulb or get something down from the top shelf in the kitchen without standing on a stepstool.

There are men who are not handy around the house: my father wasn't; my husband was only slightly better; my son John is a whiz. One out of three isn't bad. It's a stereotype that says men have to be good at fixing toaster plugs and unstopping clogged toilets while women sew on the buttons and make the porridge. If I lose a button I might as well throw the garment away. I'm three years behind in my mending.

But when one becomes a widow, suddenly the home chores become terribly important. Who's going to do them? Who's going to applaud you when you do them? It's not only that it's work you have to do yourself, it's also that there's no zest in doing it. Why bother? Do you want to put up Christmas lights this year? Do you need to put bedding plants in? Does the fence really need painting?

A lot of the inertia of grief spills over into the process of living. C.S. Lewis commented on it in his book *A Grief Observed*: "No one," he wrote, "ever told me about the laziness of grief. Except at my job – where the machine seems to run on much as usual – I loathe the slightest effort. . . . It's easy to see why the lonely become untidy."

It's not only the grass-mowing, the snow-shovelling, the broken windows, garbage, leaky faucets and eaves-troughs, sticking doors, and burnt-out light bulbs. Even more oppressive in the single-handed care and upkeep of a home are the major repairs and maintenance. It's making a decision, getting the thing done, and paying the bill – all for something you don't really care about as much anymore. Like every other problem widows face, it looms large because you're facing it alone. And there's no satisfaction in it when you do tackle a job, because who notices? Who cares?

If you think I'm giving you an argument for not owning a house, you're not completely right. Certainly I am not advising you to rush away from it. Running a house by yourself is only one more of the many challenges you face as a single person. It can be done. And there are rewards.

I have said elsewhere that you should not make any major decision – and moving would be a major one – hastily. Sit tight for at least a year, if you can, after your husband's death, while you take stock and measure your own abilities and attitudes. But don't let the house go to seed while you sit there. In the same way, you have been urged by your friends (haven't you?) not to "let yourself go," you mustn't neglect the maintenance of your home. Your house is probably your biggest single investment. Don't be afraid to spend some money on it. Take care of it. Then when you do decide to move, you'll get your money out of it.

In these heady days of the feminist movement, there are wonderful changes taking place which may make your tasks easier. There are courses springing up all over the country for women to learn how to carpenter, do electrical repairs, car maintenance, upholstery, etc., and women are taking them and learning how to cope, to their great satisfaction. I know a single woman who does all her own remodelling. If there is something she doesn't know how to do, she takes a course on the subject and learns. Her home is a showcase, an apartment in a beautiful old house, and she has done all the refinishing, carpentry, papering, painting, and electrical installations herself. A former neighbour of mine, married, took a woodworking course and built a magnificent pool table for her husband and sons. It is a work of art. The only things she bought ready-made were the balls and the cues. Now she's panelling the rec room. And there are women to whom gardening is no chore, as it is to me, who find great satisfaction in keeping their gardens glowing and beautiful. And then there are others like me who would rather have everything done for them. I'll stand by the sidelines and cheer and provide sandwiches and coffee and first aid, if necessary, for the workers. I was fortunate that my son John was handy around the house. At fourteen he took over the house, pool, and yard maintenance and I never had cause for complaint. But I realized that first summer when he went away to camp how dependent I was on him. I couldn't have done it by myself, nor did I want to.

One of the clichés of widowhood is the clingy little neighbourhood widow who needs help from her neighbours' husbands. There were times, I'll admit, when I found that help necessary. I tried to avoid criticism by inviting both husband and wife over for drinks or coffee and a snack while I explained my problem. That way I got some company and some free help, and the wife was assured that I had no designs on her husband outside of his plumbing or financial skills or whatever. There really are problems you encounter that only men can solve, but you do have to be careful how you go about asking them to solve them. Their wives resent it, and men often get the idea that that isn't the only problem you have that needs a man's touch.

But that's something else again. The point I am try-ing to make is that, ept or not, it is possible for you to go on living where you have been living and to cope by yourself. The libraries are full of how-to books, and some of them are written especially for women.

Staying on in the last home you and your husband shared together has its own kind of comfort. The pic-tures on the walls were probably discussed and hung by both of you in consultation; all the decorating decisions surrounding you were probably joint ones. A presence lingers that is sustaining. On the other hand, when and if the time comes to move, that can be good, too. As one widow said, "Moving is like closing the wound; you're healed and you move on." Take your time, though. Think about it. No rush.

I'm afraid we rushed my mother when my father died. I didn't know as much then as I do now. We thought the reasons were good and valid, but I can see now she should have had more time. Moving is a trau-matic experience and should not follow too hard on the heels of the death of one's mate. The house still retains echoes and memories which are comforting. Your mind resists change. Any decision you make is apt to be woolly-headed and unreasonable. And the inertia of the body makes one incapable of the large amounts of en-ergy required for moving.

On the other hand, it often happens now that a woman can be stranded by the death of her husband in a city that is strange to her. I myself had lived in Strat-ford only five years when Bill died. The friends we had made were obviously not lifelong friends. That can make a big difference in terms of long-term support and concern. If you find yourself in a strange community, perhaps in spite of my admonitions not to move too quickly or hastily, the best thing would be to move back to your hometown. I know two widows who did just that, both within a month of their husbands' deaths, and it was the right thing for them to do. Both of them have since remarried, by the way. I don't know if there's a moral to that story or not.

My reasons for moving were as complex as yours might be. I was tired of taking care of the house all by myself. I was tired of living in a small city, one which I discovered did not adapt easily to singles in its midst. I was tired of living in a ghetto of women, and, particularly, of widows. I felt things would be different in a larger city, and they have been. But most of all, I was tired of driving on Highway 401 to Toronto. I like driving, but not in blizzards or sleet or ice storms. And on the highway as nowhere else I was aware of the responsibility I had to take very good care of my children's only parent.

"Drive carefully," John would say as I left the house, "I don't want to live with someone else."

I was spending too much time on the highway because all my work was in Toronto. I knew I could increase my income if I moved because I would be where the work was. Driving time is unproductive time. Incidentally, a move for financial reasons such as mine is deductible.

I didn't know many widows my age but the ones I did know were affected by my decision. One of them also sold her house and moved out of town, as I did. Another put her house on the market, quit her job, took a course, and found a better job. Another stayed where she was but made envious noises and became more dissatisfied with her life. She needs another catalyst.

For many different reasons, a widow may find that the home she maintained when she was her husband's wife no longer suits her needs. It may be too expensive, too much trouble to keep up, too large as the family keeps shrinking, too empty when the widow is left alone. If enough time has passed that the reasons for moving are based on common sense and logic and not on some emotional gut reaction, then by all means move.

A move for a widow usually means a reduction in space. Whether you move from one house or apartment to another, or from a house to an apartment, the new space is usually smaller than the old space – that's part of the reason for moving, isn't it? That means getting rid of a lot of the stuff in the present space in order to fit into the new, smaller space. It means, finally, taking stock of your past, your marriage, and your possessions. And it means finding out more things about yourself. Such as, how important are possessions to you? How important is space? How much space? A garden? Neighbours? Memories? Habits?

Take your time. Consider it the biggest spring (or fall) cleaning you've ever undertaken. Go over everything. Find out what your children want, and give it to them or save it for them. Have a garage sale. Sell things or give them away, but get rid of them.

Strange reactions happen, but welcome them. This is another purge and it's valuable. I found I was reliving a future that was no longer going to occur. Things I had put away for our old age together I no longer needed, so they went out. My scenario is different; I need different props. It was not only my past I was clearing, it was also my future, and that's valuable, if somewhat painful.

We end up owning many things not by choice but by accident, because we needed something in a hurry, because someone else thought we needed something and gave it to us, because it was on sale, because it fit a room or a specific purpose at the time. How seldom it is given to anyone to choose again, or if not to choose, at least to discriminate! What you finally end up with, when you move as a widow, is what you choose to keep. Finally, and perhaps for the first time in your life, and maybe only in a negative way, your possessions make a statement about *you*.

We live in such a materialistic age; we all accumulate things like squirrels. I can't tell you what a pleasure it was to begin to divest myself of some of my possessions. I felt like Diogenes with his bowl. Remember the story of the Greek philosopher who owned nothing but a bowl in which he collected the food he begged to keep himself alive? One day he tripped and broke his bowl and he said, "At last! I'm free!" I still own too much, but I own a lot less than I did. It's nice to be lighter and freer than I was.

I had the biggest garage sale in the world, and that was a revelation in itself. I heartily recommend garage sales. People will buy anything if it's on sale, and I mean anything. There is a little paperback with complete advice on such sales, and most women's magazines have tips on them every spring. All you have to do is go to one or two and learn how for yourself. I sold tired Christmas wrap and decorations and lights, broken hockey sticks, boxes of torn sheets, threadbare towels and rags (useful for painters and mechanics, I found), toys and clothes and ornaments and glasses, old dolls with the eyes blunk out, tablecloths and placemats and utensils, clothes, appliances, furniture, carpets and lawn chairs, and my neighbour's new broom that she swept my garage floor with and left leaning against a wall. I sold my past and parts of my future that no longer existed. I'm afraid I sold some of my children's past and future, too, and I feel sorry about that.

Storage in my parents' home remained available to me until long after I was married. I didn't fully claim all my possessions until we were living in our third home. I'm sorry I couldn't grant that kind of carefree space to my children. But Liz is less of a packrat than I am, perhaps because I am one. And there's still a box of Barbie doll stuff in my apartment locker belonging to Kate.

Moving is harder on the children who are at home. I had hoped to spare them the move at least until John was finished high school, but as I became more and more busy in Toronto and unhappy in Stratford, I realized that two years out of my life at my age were more important than two years out of his life at his age, so I didn't wait. It is hard on kids to move in their teens, late in their high school years. They have no time to form new allegiances. They become aliens when it is desperately important for them to belong. I know that, and I'm sorry, and it's something you should consider if it applies. But John found a compensation in the fact that I was nicer to live with and around a lot more (instead of on the highway) once we'd moved. There are times you have to make the decision for yourself, and let the others fall into line with you.

It's a case of weighing the advantages and disadvantages. There are times when you have to cut your losses and run. You do it materially when you move. You have to take a beating on some of things you're selling off, as you might expect. You can't get much for second-hand furniture. You'll just have to consider the difference between what you paid originally and what you finally received for it as rent for the use of it. You can't take it with you – there's no room. So move on without it.

And that's what you have to do emotionally, too. You can't sit down and wither in the past. You can't wait out a future that doesn't exist. Take your memories with you, by all means, but move on.

6

The working widow

Those who do not complain are never pitied.

Jane Austen

There are about 900,000 widows in Canada, 10 per cent of women over the age of fourteen. In 1974, according to *Women in the Labour Force*, published by Labour Canada, 53 per cent of widowed, divorced, and separated women aged twenty to sixty-four were working. You could well be part of those statistics.

According to *Widows Study*, a 1971 report by the Life Underwriters' Training Council and Life Insurance Marketing and Research Association, the incomes of widows' families go down an average of 44 per cent from pre-death levels. The difference in income, before and after, is, as might be expected, in direct proportion to the size of the husband's income. There was actually an increase of 4 per cent when the family income had been less than $3,000 but also a sickening decrease of 57 per cent when the family income had been $15,000 or more. It's not surprising, in light of today's ever-increasing cost of living, to learn that almost six in ten (58 per cent) of the widows had incomes that fell below the amount required to maintain their former living standards.

And so – a lot of widows have to go to work. Trained or not, if a widow needs more money than she has coming in, she must find a means of supplementing her income. The question is what will she do? There are as many answers to that as there are people, and both are a constant source of surprise. I know one widow who has indulged a lifelong love of dolls by starting a dolls' hospital. Her painstaking, loving work is much in demand. Another widow was instrumental in starting a widows' counselling service through a local Y; she went to a community college to take the necessary courses and is now helping to run the service on a continuing, paid basis. My mother-in-law in her day took in a boarder to make ends meet. Half my baby-sitters when my children were small were older widows who turned their experience with children and their abiding interest in people into a service that is always in demand. What a widow does depends on her training, her age, her children, and her opportunities. Fortunately, at least partly because of the feminist movement, there are more opportunities than ever. Doors are opening.

But they don't open all by themselves. Neither do they present themselves as easy solutions. Remember the short story, "The Lady or The Tiger" in which the hero had to choose between two identical doors and thereby seal his fate? Well, your problem is similar when you end up at forty-plus trying to decide what to do with the rest of your life.

Rhoda Butt, special programs counsellor with the Department of Manpower and Immigration in Toronto, has conducted several successful experimental two-day workshops for the over-forty woman who wishes to re-enter the labour market. Canada Manpower Centres across Canada are ready with counsellors and expertise to help you plan your vocation and goals. Miss Butt recommends a careful assessment of your entire situation. You don't want to rush out and get a job just because you think you might need one. I mean, you could end up washing dishes in which case all you'll achieve is a change of sink. And dishpan hands.

Start by taking a good look at yourself, even before you look at the job. What are your skills? Your attitudes? Your likes and dislikes? If you can't stand talking to strangers, don't get a job as a receptionist. If you get too lonely without people, don't hide yourself in the stacks of a library. If you had a marketable skill before you were married, is it still marketable? Or do you need some brushing up – a refresher course in bookkeeping or shorthand, some practice to get your speed back at the typewriter? Some fields have changed so much that your refresher course might well take one or two years at a community college.

There is help available. I know one widow who went back for a refresher course in business at a community college. She found she qualified as a mature student. Not only did she get the course free of charge, she was also paid a nominal weekly salary (under minimum wage) to help keep her while she was bettering her job position. The government figures, rightly, that it's better to spend money on someone's education now than on her welfare later. Much more productive. My friend just landed a better-paying job.

If further training is necessary before a suitable job can be found, there are more resources available now than there ever have been. If a woman already holds a university degree she can take further courses at most colleges across Canada. Information and catalogues are available upon request from the universities. Most universities now allow credits for "life experience" to mature students; people past a certain age (usually the early twenties) are allowed to register as mature students and take courses. Ask about these when you write for catalogues and other information. Enquire, too, about bursaries, scholarships, and student loan plans.

Then there are all the community colleges that have sprung up across the country. They offer one- and two-year courses in a vast range of subjects, usually directly applicable to jobs. Most of these colleges have women's centres, specifically designed to help women in their training.

I went to a one-day conference sponsored by the Women's Centre of Humber College in Toronto. Entitled "Women on Their Own," the conference was a treasure-chest of workshops and resources all aimed at the single woman. Find out what's going on near you. The stimulation alone is going to give you fresh courage.

If you're not sure what you can do, that's all right. There are aids available such as the General Aptitude Test Battery, Creative Job Search Techniques, and Canada Manpower Training Programmes. Give Canada Manpower a call and get help.

All right, you've done your personal inventory. You are trained and ready and you know what you want to do. Now you can take a look at the job. You have to consider the built-in costs. If child-care is necessary, that is a major expense. Consider day care centres. The lack of adequate facilities to care for the children of working mothers has been one of the prongs of the feminist movement. There still is a dreadful gap between need and supply. Somehow, the needs of young children have to be met while the single mother is out earning the family bread. Often, in the case of a pre-school child, a relative or close friend or neighbour is the answer – but make it a financial arrangement if you can. It lasts longer.

There is also a difficult twilight zone in children's

ages that presents a different problem and requires a different solution. What about the children who are of school age, fairly competent, but still too young to make their own lunch, or not quite responsible enough to be at loose ends after school until someone comes home? School lunches, or again a reliable neighbour (on a paid basis to guarantee continuity), and after-school programs are all necessities in this case.

My youngest son is signed up term after term for after-school programs for which I am deeply grateful. What's more, the school allows single parents and working mothers to sign up first, showing great understanding of our pressures. Matthew may end up knowing more about macrame, cooking, ceramics, creative dance, floor hockey, and woodworking than he cares to, but I know he is constructively occupied until I get home.

There are other, personal expenses. Are you going to have to spend more on clothes to look presentable for this job? If you can't wear pantsuits at least part of the time you're going to be spending more on pantyhose (doesn't everyone use up her runned ones under pantsuits?). How far do you have to travel to get to the job? Can you afford the transportation costs? And the time it takes you to get to and from your work? Your lifestyle changes again when you take a full-time job; make sure it is a change for the better, one that you will welcome for the challenge and stimulus and not one that is going to drag you down and make you tired and more discouraged than ever.

If you take a full-time job, chances are you will have some sort of company or group policy, and chances are equally good that there is a disability clause in it. Check it out. It could be worse, at this stage of your life, if you were disabled and unable to work than if you were dead, for all practical purposes. Child support continues to be necessary no matter where you are, so be sure to find out about this.

Also, if you're working full-time, you will automatically be part of the company's Canada Pension Plan. But even part-time workers, and self-employed ones like myself, participate in the Plan – you do it at income tax time, and it's quite painless. You may, however you are involved, want to sweeten the pot a little by augmenting it through an RRSP – Registered Retirement Savings Plan – and get a tax break at the same time. You can put up to 20 per cent of your net earned income (up to certain maximums) after expenses into such a plan and that money will be untaxed in the year of investment. The tax is deferred until such time as you start to receive the money, and by that time, presumably your other income will have decreased so that you will be paying less tax on it.

It is likely, once you start working, that you will continue to do so until retirement age. This is your new vocation, beyond that of wife and mother. Take a look at your long-term goals and be sure you're going where you want to go. If you don't have any goals, maybe you should think about that, too. You're alone now. You're you. Who are you? And where are you going? What do you want? If you think I'm asking tough questions, you're right. I've been asking myself the same ones.

You have to keep on treating life as an adventure. Someone just pushed you out on a highwire and there's no safety net. Don't look down! Look ahead, and dazzle us all with your footwork. Rhoda Butt says there are fears that interfere with a successful new career. Fear of rejection. Fear of inability. Fear of competition. Fear of incompetence. Well, I'm not telling you to be unrealistic. No one expects you to *fly* off that highwire. But there's no sense being defeatist either. Don't panic. One step at a time, taken confidently, is going to get you to the other side.

Your maturity is one of your assets. No prospective

employer is going to consider you a flighty young thing who's going to drop everything as soon as she finds a man, or worry about you leaving because you're pregnant (heaven forbid!). You can offer your own stability and resolution to succeed as definite pluses. Your very need is reassuring, because it means you won't be leaving in a hurry. And some of the special emotion reserved for widows also works for you. One widow told me she felt sorry for divorcées because they were regarded as flighty; a widow with a child, on the other hand, like my friend, was pitied and revered and helped along the way.

"Remember," says Rhoda Butt, "that employers are always looking for reliable, dependable employees with the appropriate skills to fill their vacancies."

Age isn't the problem that it was (though there is still a double standard), and there are, as noted, programs designed to help the woman over forty with job training and placement. However, an older woman may not be able to develop a marketable skill or she may find that she lacks the energy to work full-time. Some of the temporary help firms may be able to place her. Or consider this:

I have mentioned baby-sitters already, and sitting is a friendly, human way to earn extra money. But housekeeping is even more so. Every woman who has run a home of her own has a skill that she can consider selling. Unfortunately in North America today, people tend to look down on housekeepers or maids or "hired help." But they are worth their weight in gold and in very short supply. If you are alone, or have very few ties, you might consider taking on an adopted family. The pay is good, the expenses are nil, and there's built-in company. You'll actually work less than you did as mistress of your own household – there are rules about slave labour which, of course, don't apply to wives. Think about it.

For those women past retirement age who want to

71

keep busy, paid or not, because time hangs heavy on their hands, volunteer jobs have become more and more interesting and challenging. Volunteers are much in demand and are always welcomed.

If you lack the energy to do volunteer work on a regular basis, but would still love to do something if only to keep up with other human beings, there are still things you can do.

Perhaps you have a skill that is of use to someone. When I was first married, the dean of women at my college asked me if I would help some newly arrived Chinese students who were having trouble with idiomatic English. My husband was taking a night course, so my students came to me on the night he was out, and we launched on their indoctrination. I did it for nothing, that is, no money, but I gained a great deal from it. I made new friends. You could do that. If you were a teacher, or even if you weren't, you could discuss the vagaries of our silly language with some young new Canadians, and you might even offer them some comforting advice about survival while you're at it.

The old golden rule still applies. When you're feeling rotten yourself, try to reach out to help someone else who feels rotten. You'll feel better making them feel better. There are still things you can do for other people which will make you feel valuable and useful. There are a lot of shut-ins now, right across the country, and some of them are on accessible lists. The Meals on Wheels organizations have such lists; nursing homes have waiting lists, government welfare organizations have lists. Ask if you can volunteer to phone a few people, keep in touch with them, check on their health, chat and gossip and spend the time of day with them – by telephone. You can still talk, can't you? Reach out with your electronic tongue and help someone else. It's perfectly possible to make a good friend by voice alone.

There are several helpful hints I can pass on to a working widow which, like everything else in these scattered pages, I found out the hard way. The first is that you're going to get tired, tired as you have never been. There are times when it will seem that there is no respite. You will have gone the second mile and still there is no haven in sight. Well, weariness is like pain in many respects: you have to give in to it. Ride with it. Don't be ashamed to crawl into bed after dinner. Sometimes an hour is all you need. Sometimes it pays to go to bed early and stay there until morning.

There are so many times when you have to keep on working, running as you do from the job, the paying one, to another, the cooking and bottle-washing one, that it would be wise to recognize the times when you can afford to goof off. Who says the sheets have to be changed every Saturday, or whenever you used to change them? All the rules laid down in domestic science books and the women's magazines were written for someone else, someone with more time, more leisure, more devotion to good housekeeping than you now have – and more money. So what if the place doesn't get dusted as often? No one pays anything, even attention, to a dusty coffee table. If you're a compulsive housekeeper, then of course you're going to ignore my advice, but if you are feeling guilty because you're not doing what you think someone else thinks you should be doing, then forget it.

I'm not recommending that you turn into a slob. What I am trying to do is absolve you from compulsive housekeeping. I used to be a compulsive housekeeper. I like to call myself a comfortable one now. My aim is to create a comfortable home for my family, not a showcase for other people.

One of the sad, ironic advantages of having no husband is that there is no one you think you are failing when you are less than perfect. You're not disappointing anyone if the place isn't spotless by 5 P.M. each day. It's unlikely that your children will even notice. I do have one terribly tidy child, grown now, who, when she comes home to visit, tidies everything in sight until it's out of sight. I can't find anything for days after she's gone. If you have one of these and it's live-in, bear with it and be grateful. Your home will never look like a disaster area.

Guilt, it seems, is an occupational hazard of being a woman. One of the things that is going to happen to you, as you rush about doing what is uppermost and demands to be done, is that you will feel guilty about the less demanding things, including children, that just wait there to be attended to. I'm a prime sufferer myself. I always feel guilty if my kids are working and I'm not, though I find they don't seem to feel at all guilty when I'm up and about and they are stretched out in front of the television set.

If you feel guilty, as I do, about how different, how much more comfortable and secure their lives might be if you weren't working and neglecting them, stop it. The if-onlies can take you right back to Self-Pity, maudlin variety. Life isn't the same, it never will be, and all the if-onlies in the world won't change it. Be grateful you have your children and think of what character they're building. You're building a little character yourself, and you're going to need it because women live a long time. Alone.

A little healthy neglect really doesn't hurt a child, not if he learns independence. Bake a pan of brownies once in a while as an unlooked-for bonus. Chocolate addicts like my kids never feel neglected when they're eating brownies.

On the other hand, you musn't feel like a martyr. It's not only bad for your character, it's also very hard to live with. Give your kids a break as well as yourself. Don't set impossibly high standards that no one can live up to. Break down, have a little fun once in a while. It'll do you all good.

Your ego is something that you as a widow have to be careful of. It tends to wither, like a flower without sunshine. You have no one to tell you when you're doing a good job or, for that matter, when you're being a darn fool. Lack of feedback can be very damaging to the psyche. You lose your self-image. That's why, whether it's necessary or not, it's actually valuable to a newly single person to go to work. Work guarantees contact with other people. Work can be the biggest morale-lifter you can find. Work provides focus, a chance to get out of the silent house, to become a functioning independent human being in your own right. "Work keeps at bay three great evils," wrote Voltaire, "boredom, vice, and need." A widow would do well to keep all three at bay.

Once in a while, unbidden, a feeling of accomplishment will arise, and this enables you to square your shoulders and keep on keeping on. There's nothing wrong with a little healthy self-congratulation every now and then. It's a whole lot better than guilt. No one ever said you had to be superlady, but once in a while you feel like it. Go ahead. You're entitled.

7

Children

Ring around a rosie,
A pocket full of posies,
Husha, husha.
We all fall down.

Nursery rhyme

Even in this day and age, protected as we are from death, children know about it, sing about it, play games with it, honour it. This nursery rhyme comes from the time of the Black Death when sniffing a posy was believed to offer protection against the unseen killer which decimated the population of Europe in the fourteenth century. "We all fall down," of course, means we all die. And we all do, sooner or later.

I believe that adults have no right to hide death from children. It is a terrible thing to lie to them.

I was seven when my grandfather died and I knew nothing about it. One day I was taken to see grandma's new home, a comfortable apartment, but there was no room for grandpa and no sign of him either.

"What about grandpa?" I remember asking. "Where will he sleep?" And I was told that grandpa had gone away on a long trip and wouldn't be back. What a rotten thing to do, running out on grandma like that! And it was so unlike him. That wasn't fair, not to tell me. I don't remember how old I was before I finally realized grandpa was dead. By the time I knew, he was a fading memory and I was robbed of awe and grief at his death.

Surely with the death of someone as close as a father, there can be no avoidance of the fact. But how well it is handled depends on the age of the child and on the emotional health of the mother. One week after Bill's death, on the Sunday, I drove the children out to the cemetery after church just so we could check in private on what we had left in a crowd at the funeral. The flowers were dead and there was no tombstone.

"Well, there it is," I said. "You see, he's not here. His body is here and we pay it respect."

I do believe that, but I am reminded of a passage in Pearl Buck's book *A Bridge For Passing*, about the death of her husband, in which she recalled her mother's grief at the death of Pearl's brother. A friend said something about the body being merely the earthly remains, that the child's spirit was safe in heaven. And Pearl's mother replied that the body was all she had left, the body she had borne and nursed and cared for. She has a point. Bill is not in the cemetery; he's closer to me at home, or anywhere I go. But oh, how I miss that body!

Anyway, we didn't have the body to gaze at. We had a muddy pile of earth. Everyone nodded silently at what I had said, and they all looked suitably respectful. We were dry-eyed. Kate broke the silence with a question:

"What's his address?"

We all laughed. Bless her!

"Range 16, lot 43," I said, and we were released.

Laughter can be just as valid a cry of anguish as

tears. It's easier (sometimes) to laugh than it is to cry, and it's much more socially acceptable. I know that, but where did my children learn it so young? Laughter is a mask for pain. Sometimes laughter enables you to get closer to the hurtful point than tears ever will. Tears soften and blunt the edges of pain; that's why they are so useful and must be welcomed when they come.

Crying helps. Help your children to cry. Girls and boys. Maybe especially boys, because there still is this stigma attached to masculine tears that they must be helped over. Tears are still the safest release. I'm not saying you have to drown in them, but a few moist eyes early on can brighten the vision later. Help your children to deal with strong feelings. Help them to cry. But laughter makes reality bearable – in short doses – until reality can be faced altogether.

Between the ages of three and five there is an inability to understand death, to conceive of it as a permanent thing. You will be required to give the facts, and to keep on giving them, for as long as the child must hear them. It is a crucial age at which to lose a parent. In a study by psychiatrist Dr. Michael Rutter, reported in Sula Wolff's book *Children Under Stress*, it was found that "the loss of a parent at three or four years is especially damaging because this is the time at which parents are most needed as models for identification."

Somewhere you will have to find a role model for your young sons, perhaps your own brother, if you have one, or brother-in-law, or a cousin, or your father, or a friend of your husband's. At whatever age, sons are terribly vulnerable to their widowed mothers. You must start early to distance yours enough to stand free of you.

Sula Wolff also writes, however, "that the death of a mother generally leads to a greater disruption of the family than the death of a father." If you've been getting the subliminal message from some people that the wrong person died (yes, that too!) tell them that.

Between the ages of five and nine, children develop a gradual acceptance of death as a permanent thing that happens to everyone. They will still want to talk about it a lot. Don't change the subject. Explain the facts. Be open and honest about the cause of death. They will be less frightened than if you shroud it in secrecy.

At this age a child might harbour some feelings of guilt if he or she was ever angry at the deceased. Children have a very direct apprehension of cause and effect and have been known to blame themselves for a death in the family, especially a sudden death, and especially if, in the few weeks before the death, they happened to have shouted in anger: "I hate you. I wish you were dead." Guilt and fear may get all mixed up in their heads, and you'll have to help them over it. It's important to talk about it.

Then, too, children may feel anger at being left. Why not? Lots of mothers feel angry at being left. It helps to talk about it. He didn't mean to go away and leave you. He couldn't help it. Don't blame him.

And if by chance he did mean it, if he committed suicide, then you still mustn't be angry. Help the children to feel sympathy for the pain and despair and anguish that forced him to such an act. Don't blame him.

But don't blame God either. If you have a faith, find a way to explain death (and life) without implicating God as the villain. If you have honest doubts, express them. Don't be afraid to say, "I don't know." How fortunate you are if you have a strong faith and can communicate your belief to your children!

"God needed him." Have you heard that line? Or – and this is worse – "God punished him." You might not say that one, but pray that your children don't overhear someone else saying it. Death is not a punishment for sin. *Everyone dies*. Make sure your children understand that.

By the time they're older, children may not turn so freely to their mother to discuss their father's death. It's important that you keep on talking about him – easily and naturally and lovingly. No one else will. People don't seem to want to talk about someone after he dies. It's as if the earth had swallowed him up and he never existed at all. Well, if he didn't exist, where did all these children come from? Stay open. Be accessible. Make sure your children understand that they can talk if they want to talk. Talk a lot. Keep on talking, whatever age they're at. And remember this: Children need large doses of tender loving care.

So do mothers.

Now, having gotten all soft and mushy, let me warn you not to be too soft. Don't cling. Don't smother. Especially your sons. Sula Wolff warns of this: "Clinging mothers, especially to sons, impede the child's growing up process. Some sons can be handicapped by it, too concerned for the widowed mother." Sometimes you have to discourage their concern for you.

One Saturday night that first summer, it happened that both the girls were out, Matt was invited to a friend's for the night, and John was going to a movie. He was the last one out of the house and hesitated as he said goodbye, realizing in the same instant that I would be alone for the evening.

"Would you rather I stayed home?" he asked.

"That's the last thing I want," I said. "Get out of here." You have to do that. In a way, in time, you have to become less of a mother.

It's called being androgynous and it goes hand in hand with becoming the breadwinner, the head of the house, the decision-maker. As you develop your so-called "masculine" qualities of energy, independence, aggressiveness, you will tend to repress the feminine. That's what I mean when I say you become less of a mother. You have to become both mother and father to your children. Again, it isn't easy.

If, however, you have troubles with your children that you feel you cannot handle, there are experts who can help you when the printed word fails and you desperately need to talk to someone. Start with the teacher, if your child is of school age. The teacher knows the kid better than anyone and may be able to help you with your problem. Try your minister, or Sunday School teacher, if you are a regular church attender, or the Scoutmaster or Brown Owl, if your child attends such a group.

You will discover how very kind other people can be. Different friends have taken my younger son to the Father and Son Banquet at Scouts each year. Both boys' camp directors have been wonderfully kind and helpful. Matt's Big Brother is a joy and a wonder. In fact, the Big Brothers movement is a joy and a wonder, reaching out as it does to help fatherless boys between the ages of six and sixteen. There are times when, as a single parent, you find it impossible to be in two places at once. That's when friends from many sources step into the breach and help. If never before, you learn to receive gratefully and to say thank you from the bottom of your heart.

If you have a son under sixteen years of age do try to get a Big Brother for him. The time he gives to your son is valuable to you in more ways than one. When you are responsible for everything your children do, the relief you feel when someone else takes over, if only for a couple of hours, has to be experienced as it cannot be described. The Big Brother may become the role model your child needs and that's really important.

Don't, whatever you do, hold up their missing father as the model your children must live up to. That's blackmail. Don't ever say, "Your father would be disappointed in you." Don't even hint that the child is not living up to his non-existent father's expectations of him. There is no answer a child can give to that and you have saddled him with guilt and posthumous resentment that he can't get rid of. The only way I conjure up their dead father to my children is in a positive way. I say, "Your father would be proud of you," or, "He'd be happy to see you doing so well."

Tempting as it may be, don't tell your son that he's the man of the house now. Other people will anyway, so you don't have to emphasize it. He'll feel his responsibility keenly as it is; try not to rush him out of childhood any faster than he has already been pushed.

Your children necessarily will assume more responsibility in their lives than they might have. They will be on their own sooner and they will be doing more for themselves – and for you. I can say don't burden your older children with too much responsibility but it's hard not to. Certainly there is added pressure on them if you have to work to supplement your income. You must rely on your children's co-operation. The danger is that you will lean on them too heavily. Kids are kids and they still have to be respected as such. Sure, they'll pitch in and put dinner in the oven, make a salad, set the table, run errands to the store, clean up after a meal or help with the cleaning and laundry, and God bless them for it. But don't ask them to make the decisions, plan the menus, or remember what to do without written memory jogs. Or hang up their clothes.

What about money? What provision is there for your dependent children in the event of your death before they are ready to leave the nest? Is your income dependent upon your life or is it in trust or investments that are available to your family as well? Certainly your job income will cease if you should die now, and so would your husband's survivor's pension payable to the widow only. If too many sources were to dry up, then you should consider some insurance to keep your children afloat.

Give a thought to their education, if you can. I gave thought to it, but very little money. In widows' surveys this was the area that altered most dramatically with the death of the father. The fact is that your children will bear more or most, if not all, of the cost of their education themselves. Ontario has a system of student loans and grants that is in the process of revision. Enquire in your province about similar loans and ask at the universities and colleges about the bursaries, loans, grants, scholarships – whatever is available. Psychologists have proved that anxiety and tension improve learning ability – another ironic advantage.

We have already recognized the fact that bereavement is usually accompanied by a substantial drop in income. This can affect children in more ways than the obvious one. They are deprived not only of some of the material benefits they had when their father was alive but also of a great deal of their mother's time. Because in her attempts to fill in the money gap she runs out of time for them. There is less money for toys and treats and trips but there is also less time for inexpensive pleasure outings and for bedtime stories, homework help, and games. In other words, no one is having any fun, least of all you.

That's one of the sadder continuing facts of widowhood. You're not having any fun any more. The person who made life most interesting for you and with whom you most liked to have fun is gone. No one else is going to go out of his way to see that you have any fun. So you're going to have to manufacture your own.

Your children are going to feel the same way. Not only is half the source of their comfort, well-being, and fun gone, but the one who's left is a lot more sour and serious than they ever remember her being. Small wonder. You were never scared and lonely before. Well, share your loneliness with the kids. Take time to go on a picnic with them, or to a movie, or to have Chinese food sent in, whatever. Do a jigsaw puzzle, go for a bike ride or cross-country skiing, make popcorn, watch a TV show together, explore a new park. Your solutions need not be expensive. They just have to be done together. You'll find that your children are delightful people to be with, and it's so very comforting to be with people who really love you – very good for the soul and the ego.

Do something else for your children. Have a party. It's good therapy for you and it's good psychology for them. Show them that good times can still happen, even though their father is gone. Have a family sleighride, or take a bunch of kids tobogganing or skating and bring them back for hot apple cider and hamburgers or lasagna or something. Or have a backyard barbecue in the summer.

Show your children that you care. Listen to them. Do not judge – "That's a terrible thing to say!" Do not stifle them – "You mustn't think things like that!" Help them to articulate their feelings. Recognize anger if it exists and help them to talk it out. Fear too.

It was several months before Kate and I confessed to each other that every time we burped we waited for eight minutes to see if we would die. Sudden death can leave residual fear like that. Death can happen so easily. You have to learn to trust life again, and help your children to trust, too. Death is not necessarily catching.

Perhaps all of us felt the apprehension that Matthew voiced. He was nervous about leaving me to go back to school the day after the funeral. He was afraid, I guess, that I might drop dead, too, and what was there in his experience to say this might not happen? We all took an extra day off together before we parted to resume our lives again.

Matt is in a Special Education class. I phoned his teacher and warned her of his fear. She discussed his situation with the other children in the class and tried to prepare them for a normal reception of him. It was too much to expect. Not knowing what to say, they said nothing, and avoided him. He came home feeling like a social outcast. Grownups also do that, too, say nothing, because they don't know what to say. It's better to speak. Words don't lie as heavy in the air as silence does.

There was only one child who broke the boundaries of fair play with Matt, and I guess he had problems of his own.

"Yah, yah," he shouted at Matt one day. "I'm better than you. I have a father and you don't. Yah, yah." That's unanswerable. (But I have the feeling that some women think that about me and my lack of a husband.)

Children, in short, will go through the same stages of shock, rage, fear, and withdrawal that their bereaved mother does. If you can help them through it, you will perhaps not only shorten their mourning period, you may also help yourself. As a widow, of course, you are harder hit than your children. You have lost the companion of your life, your mate, your lover, your best friend (haven't you?). Your grief will affect the whole household, and will continue to do so when you have attacks of it.

Oddly enough, however, or perhaps not oddly at all, just as a widow who has survived an unhappy marriage will be more badly affected by the death of her husband, so will her children be less able to handle the bereavement. Again, it is the grief and guilt of the mother that affect the children. If you have such a problem you'll have to work out your hostility for the sake of your own mental health, but I pray that you do not turn your hostility on the children. They need you, as whole and loving as you can be.

You must learn to share with your children – your sorrow, satisfactions, some of your worries, your self – without leaning on them too heavily. Their lives have changed, too; you can't protect them from the world any more. The world has already happened to them. Go ahead and communicate with them, and expect a lot. They can deliver more help, common sense, and practical solutions than you could have imagined. Just don't frighten them. You're the adult; keep it that way. You make the decisions, inform them of your plans but don't expect them to plan for you. You can't opt out that easily. You're the head of the household now. Act like it.

Now if I sound awesomely tough and mature, let me quickly confess that there have been many times when I have broken down and been the recipient of comfort from my children. My youngest leaves his place at the table and comes and pats my arm if he sees weather warnings in me. In the first weeks and months when I continued to try to take the walks Bill and I were accustomed to taking on Sunday afternoons, Matt would leave his friends and run after me to tag along. And the older children would spot my lonely times and one or the other of them would wander into the living room and offer to talk. I have learned more about electronics and stereo equipment and physics from John than I care to know. But they also help more with chores than they ever did and provide companionship as well as assistance. There is a kind of bittersweet compensation in this. They don't have to share me with my husband any more. Perhaps that is a saving grace, that although they no longer have two parents, they now have access to the undivided attention of one – when they can catch me.

One other thing I have to bring up: dating. That is an old-fashioned word, and there is much more said about it in another chapter, but you should give a thought to how it affects the children because it will in turn affect

86

you. Little children often feel threatened by their mother's dating. They are afraid she will be taken away from them, or else they resent a father figure, if the man in question attempts to come on too strong as an authority. Teenaged children feel threatened too, particularly a boy who regards himself in some way as the man of the house.

As for Mother, she feels like an overgrown teenager herself. Very odd. I mean, theoretically, you can stay out as late as you want because you're grownup and you don't have a curfew, but can you really face your kids if you stay out till four in the morning? I can't. I'm still the Mother.

Children older than mine feel somewhat proprietary about their widowed mothers. A few I have spoken to are genuinely happy for their parent when she finds another interest, whether it's a round-the-world cruise, a good job, or a new husband. But many adult children are fearful that a new man in their mother's life is merely after her money – I mean, he couldn't possibly be interested in her in a man-woman relationship, could he? (He could.) The commonest reaction to a new man is a well-hidden, latent jealousy. An older widow's decision to remarry can bring back painful memories of the bereavement that left her thus available. As long as she was faithful to her husband's memory, father was still around, in a way. Even at this late stage in life, a son or daughter may feel rejected by the mother's insistence on having a life of her own. If any of these reactions occur in your life, you will find they're harder to deal with than with the bewildered grief of a five-year-old. But you will have to deal with the problem. All I can say is, keep the lines of communication open.

Your relationship with your grown children is at once a personal and a contemporary problem. The extended family of past generations is no longer popular.

Widowed grandmothers and maiden aunts and dotty uncles and spinster sisters used to live together and share the child care and chores with the mother and father in houses big enough to accommodate all of them. Daughters and sons today are not too eager to have a widowed mother live with them in smaller quarters, and she is often fiercely independent and wants to do for herself in her own place as long as she can. According to Hope Holmstead, chairman of the Advisory Council on Aging, "Canada has the highest per capita rate of persons in institutions" – the aged among them. It's not an enviable record, nor an ideal situation. What can I say? What can you do? Your arrangements will depend on your financial situation, your health, and your relationship with your children.

"It's harder for older widows," an older widowed aunt wrote to me, "than for young ones, for you are still needed. That is the most difficult adjustment to make – to have no one to whom you are absolutely essential." She is right. I am lucky that I have not yet been left alone, but I know the time is coming. There have been many times already when I have been aware that I need my children more than they need me, and I know I must not let that need overwhelm them. If I seem at this point to be suggesting more problems than I can solve, the fault is not in me but in the situation we find ourselves in. It's a bind.

Two of my children have left home now, and the other two will probably be away at school by the time this book is published. I'm beginning to feel like the last of the Ten Little Indians. But I have not been as disturbed by the departure of the fledglings from the nest as other women I know. One mother said to me when our first daughters went off to college: "Isn't it terrible, that empty place at the dinner table?" I didn't remind her I already had an empty place.

I have not been as disturbed because I have this larger departure I am still coping with. At least my children are still on this earth. I can phone them and they can visit and I can talk to them. And hug them. That helps.

What you do for your children is what you must do for yourself. Face the facts. Reality hurts, but hiding from it is going to hurt more in the long run. Share your sorrow. Support each other in your grief. Your children, no matter what their ages, are the only people in the world who come close to knowing how bad it is, who have a loss almost as deep as yours. Care for them and share yourself. If you can, share faith and hope as well. Assert your faith by making an effort. Try to make things *better* for your children because of the insight you've gained. Love them and thereby honour the person whose loss you share.

8

Companionship

So far as is known,
no widow ever eloped.

E.W. Howe

In Scarlett O'Hara's day, widows knew what was expected of them. They wore black up to their throats and sat in the parlour with the other widows creating garments with their nimble fingers and destroying reputations with their equally nimble tongues. We're not as trapped as Scarlett was in her widow's weeds and her completely circumscribed life. On the other hand, there aren't many Rhett Butlers around these days.

The first time I went to a dance without an escort I thought of Scarlett O'Hara and her tippy-tappy widowed feet. My local ratepayers' association in Stratford, which I served as a member of the executive (all the females on the executive were widows – we were posthumous tokens) had its annual dinner dance, another widow and I were drafted to man the door and take tickets. That was okay; everyone who came in had to speak to us. We treated our table to wine at dinner, as a means of thanking the gallants who supplied us with drinks during the evening.

But after dinner, when the floor was cleared and the orchestra started up, the two of us were left, wallflowers for the night. Our president, vice-president, and treasurer each danced a duty dance with us. Close friends and neighbours whirled by without a thought.

That's when I started to formulate a few of Widow Wylie's Rules for Lorn Widows. Number One is *don't cluster*. If you do have to go to a party or a meeting or an exhibit or a rally or whatever without an escort, go alone or with another couple but not in the company of a gaggle of women. The old rule of teenage days still holds: boys are scared off by groups of girls.

It's hard at first going out alone, but after a while you get used to it and you may find you prefer to be a free agent. If you're having a rotten time, you can leave without consulting anyone else; if you're having a great time, you can stay on. Sometimes it's handy to take a cab to a party – who knows who will drive you home?

Now, as to parties, a little strategy is in order. It's more than the transportation. You have to consider your clothes. There is a subtle difference between male-escorted clothes and single independent clothes. For one thing, if you're driving yourself, you'd better wear something practical and sturdy in which you can drive, and park the car, and walk to your destination. Then too, if you're going alone, you can't wear clothes that are an open invitation to every man there. I mean, even if you are open, you want to be more subtle than that. Also, you have to consider the other women there.

So here's another Wylie Rule: *the smaller the party the more discreet the clothes*. At small parties you want to remain friends with the other women, so don't compete; at large parties, on the other hand, if you're not a little conspicuous, who's going to notice you? It pays to advertise. Just make sure the product is class.

The next rule, at least for dances, is *find someone of your own to go with*. That way you have a built-in partner – for the evening – someone to trade off with the other women for dancing. And it makes everyone more comfortable about seating arrangements. (Everyone assumes that people come in pairs and they must be seated boy-girl, boy-girl.)

There is another stereotype of widows, older even than the cloistered image of Scarlett O'Hara's day. Widows down through the ages have been considered sex-starved and therefore sex-mad. And men down through the ages, especially the married ones, have felt it incumbent upon themselves to offer to service the old girls, give them a lift, a therapeutic shot of what they've been missing.

It might be interesting to note in passing that the pitch is different in the case of a divorcée. Whereas the attitude to the widow is "You need this," the attitude to a divorcée is "You must be an easy lay." Not much to choose between them, actually, as far as one's self-esteem is concerned.

I'd heard of these sexual social workers, friends' husbands who figure old George's wife needs a little servicing now that he's gone and who are willing to lend themselves to a good cause. I was braced for that, though unable to believe that it would actually happen. I was right. It didn't happen. My friends' husbands have been discretion itself, and kindness, offering me drinks and financial advice upon request and at most a friendly hug or a discreet kiss on the cheek when farewells were in order.

Nevertheless, all the clichés about the offers widder-women get from helpful, obliging, and usually married males are true. It is also a time-worn cliché that they'll get a warm welcome.

92

He that would woo a maid must feign, lie and flatter,
But he that woos a widow must down with his
britches and at her.

Nathaniel Smith wrote that in 1669!

Widows are vulnerable and men know it. The first time I had hands laid on me in lust, and not in love, it took me a while to know the difference. I mistook the first arms and shoulders offered to me after my husband's death for comfort with no strings attached. What really surprised me was the warmth of my response, through the tears, something no widow I knew had warned me about. One hears of the passes made and the invitations offered but one seldom learns of the passes completed and the offers accepted. Maybe it's time someone talked about that. Maybe there *is* reason for the wives to keep their husbands away from their widowed friends!

Anyway, the next rule is *stay away from your friends' husbands*. Consider yourself every family's maiden aunt, friendly but frigid. That way you'll keep getting invited back.

If you're going to maintain a social life, sooner or later you are going to have to reciprocate. Even with the natural winnowing process I have mentioned elsewhere, whereby old friends seem to forget you at the dinner table, others, often unexpected, will have found you interesting enough for other reasons to put you on their guest lists. It's time to start entertaining again.

If you're nervous about it, you're not alone. Your friends are too. One of the first couples I had to visit early on kept expecting Bill to appear. My friend went to get glasses and told me months later she automatically got four. Other friends get nervous when you serve the drinks; the men always think they should do it. And they don't like you to leave them for long while you putter in the kitchen. There's no one to spell you off while you're gone. To offset this, I have developed what I call a *There!* kind of entertaining. I don't care how much work I have to do beforehand but the food has to be completely ready before the guests arrive. Then all I have to do is carry it on.

"There!" I say, and it is. No one has to carve, or serve, or toss, or fuss about you slaving over a hot stove.

This kind of food makes for lovely relaxed parties, by the way. All the food goes on the table at once, as for example, with a Danish smorgasbord, or a fondue bourguignonne, a Mongolian hot pot, or an Aiolian provençal meal, and people can eat and drink and talk to their heart's content without budging. I do ask someone, usually the man on my right, to look after the wine, and someone else to carve – if there is any carving to do. People like to feel needed and helpful, especially if they don't have to do all that much to get the feeling.

The other crunchy time for your friends comes when they leave. They feel they should stay and help you clean up. Shoo them out. Other times are much worse than this. They're just not aware of them.

One nice thing about being grownup, having a home of your own, and being able to cook, is that you can invite a man for dinner, or a drink before, or a nightcap after. And a casual lunch in or out with a male friend, no matter who suggested it, isn't going to end up with complications. (Albert, there is no tomorrow – then how about this afternoon?) Men get lonely, too. Be kind – but not *that* kind!

Truth told, what a widow really misses is the cuddling and the comfort, rather than sex. If sex is part of the package and the only way she can get the other, then sometimes she buys it, and sometimes in her need she calls it love.

"Love," wrote Bertrand Russell, "is something far

more than desire for sexual intercourse, it is the principal means of escape from the loneliness which afflicts most men and women throughout the greater part of their lives." Even married people.

You're looking for a friend, not a lover. Friend first, anyway. Women who are alone miss male companionship. There is something refreshing and different about the male viewpoint and expertise, or we think there is. "We have to consider," as feminist writer Gloria Steinem points out, "to what extent we are all man junkies."

Here's another rule that women of my age have to learn: *throw away your 1950s stereotypes about males and females*. And throw away, while you're at it, the red-hot fifties lover who gives lines instead of human responses. You are a female human being, not a girl, chick, dame, broad, or babe. If you never were *friends* with men before, start now. A lot of them aren't used to it, but it's good for them. You, too. There's still a strong hold on the old double standard. If they're over a certain age, women still expect to sit and wait to be called, never to be the aggressor or initiator, never to be merely friendly (just like one of the boys), and never to go to bed with anyone for the sake of comfort and companionship – it has to be called love. Feminist thinking has made some inroads among younger women, but older widows find it difficult to do anything but sit and wait like Rapunzel to be asked to let down their hair. My generation, give or take ten years, was brought up to believe in the knight-on-the-white-charger who would come and take us away from all this. The some-day-my-prince-will-come syndrome is not only very hard on women but a terrible responsibility for men. Single again, widows find it a temptation to sit down among the ashes, Cinderella once more, waiting for the pumpkin to turn into a coach and to be whisked off to the ball again.

Here's the key question: Would you like to live with someone again? Samuel Johnson, commenting on a man who remarried shortly after his mate in an unhappy marriage had died, said that it was a "triumph of hope over experience." How hopeful are you? Granted, companionship and sex are two different things, but marriage is something else again.

If it's any reassurance, the statistical odds are against you, in spite of Jackie and Betty Kennedy. Only one in ten widows remarry. Well-meaning friends have told you (haven't they?) that you will get married again in a few years, as if that were the solution to all your problems. You know it isn't. Married people have problems, too. But you have to realize that widows are a glut on the market. Everyone may assume that you'll get married again, but you mustn't assume that. As with your insurance policies, you must consider your options. Marriage is merely one of them, perhaps the least likely.

But you should think about it. Work your way through it and come to a decision so that you are whole and secure within yourself. Think about whether you want to risk your emotions and your life on another marital venture. One widow wrote me, "I have not yet met a man with whom I want to spend more than three or four hours – the length of time it takes to eat a good dinner."

I know it's fear. My own wound is still so raw I am terrified of what another loss could do to me. I think I can stand anything, and I can, but why put myself out for such pain? I found that my feeling has been duly recognized by psychiatrists. It is called a "phobic response to marriage" and is experienced by women who lost their mates without warning. It affects the nature of eventual recovery. Yes.

But you still need companionship. Fortunate are you if you can find someone who will be satisfied with the lemonade kisses and milk-and-water hugs of your youth, that is, a platonic companion. And fortunate, too, if that's all *you* want. Try as one will to live a spiritual life, one still has a physical body that is comforted by human contact. It's another of the inexorable problems of widowhood that must be dealt with. Obviously, you're not going to be able to live with yourself in a state of promiscuity (are you?) but you have this devastating hunger . . .

You're going to be all right. Bertrand Russell suggests that women will atrophy and become brittle if they give up sex after having had it for years. David Reuben (of *Everything You Always Wanted to Know About Sex* fame) says much the same thing. They're both talking nonsense. There is nothing to get rusty, or brittle, for that matter. If your general health is good, so are your moving parts. You'll be able to deliver if and when you want to. But your own needs must be recognized. Why do you think older widows lavish so much love and affection on their dogs or cats? And baby-sit, and teach Sunday School, and go to church? All these are acceptable ways of letting off – and receiving – love.

Hugs and kisses are available closer to home when you still have children there. I ask for it, for loving. My older son, at fourteen, was embarrassed the first time I asked him to give me a hug. Matthew, my younger son, never had any problem because he had never stopped. And my daughters' shoulders seemed at times too young for the burden of grief I was laying on them. But my need for physical reassurance was strong and I got my hugs. I think it's good for the children. Two of mine are not demonstrative by nature but they can handle a swift hug with a great deal more aplomb now. Perhaps it will be a helpful expertise in the future. And it helps to sublimate a need.

Sublimate, according to the dictionary, means "to

convert the energy of primitive impulses into acceptable social and cultural manifestations." Fortunately these days a lot more manifestations are acceptable than ever used to be! It's more likely that the limits of your behaviour lie within you and not in the acceptance of society around you.

You still have to convert that energy and find an outlet for those impulses. Exercise helps, in more ways than one. Regular exercise is going to keep you fit and healthy into your old age, for you need every resource you can lay your hands on. *Join a club or a Y, take yoga classes, pursue a sport on your own.* Just make sure that you get enough good, hard, regular exercise to convert that energy. If you ever do decide that sublimation is for the birds, you'll find you have stamina for other things also.

Cherish your friends. I am a closer, better friend to a lot of people than I ever was in my married life. I need them, and they have made room for me in their lives. But I try to give in return. Marriage, you see, isn't the only close relationship you can have.

Widowhood, it seems, is becoming a complete personality course. A finishing school? As you gather all your resources you become a more complete, self-fulfilling person, never a bad thing. You gain strength, and perspective, and new, wider, extended friendships. And the best new friend you have is yourself.

9

Loneliness

There are days when solitude for someone my age is a heady wine that intoxicates you with freedom, others when it is a bitter tonic, and still others when it is a poison that makes you beat your head against the wall. . . . This evening I would much prefer not to say which it is; all I want is to remain undecided, and not to be able to say whether the shiver that will seize me when I slip between the cold sheets comes from fear or contentment.

Colette

Loneliness is an increasing problem today and is not confined to widows. The high mobility of our society has made deep and lasting friendships difficult to make and maintain. If a couple doesn't have each other, they're in trouble, and frequently they are, as the increasing fragmentation of the family makes clear. There is no doubt, however, that intimate relationships alleviate loneliness.

We all know that. We also know that the relationships have to be creative and supportive and based on genuine affection, or they will be damaging. Still, drowning people clutch at straws. It is loneliness that causes a lot of so-called promiscuity among single people (and not only singles!). Sex can provide a short-term spurious intimacy that begins by comforting and ends by alienating people even more. The moral is that we all need love.

This book is really about love. Death wouldn't mean anything if you hadn't loved the one who died. And you are not going to survive now if you do not withdraw that love and aim it elsewhere. Your first target is yourself. If you don't love and accept yourself, you're not going to be able to love others, and you're going to go on being lonely.

First you have to find out who you are. You've been someone else all your life. You were your parents' daughter, your husband's wife, your children's mother. Now you are your own keeper, and a survivor. In spite of all the kindnesses of well-meaning friends and relatives, the one thing they can't do for you is make you grow. In fact, they have a tendency to make you become less than you could be, precisely because they are so kind and well-meaning.

When you lose your husband, you lose your best friend and your sternest critic as well. Lots of people tell you when you look nice, when you've done a good job, when your dessert is delicious, or what a good speech you made. But few people care enough to tell you when you've been a horse's ass. They just let you go on making a fool of yourself. Surely you did that for each other, rode herd, provided a system of checks and balances, offered constructive criticism, blew the whistle when it was time? I hope you did. And that's what you miss when you don't have it any more – feedback. You have to learn to look at yourself.

Know yourself. It's an ancient Greek saw, and it still has a few teeth. Take a good long look at yourself. Pain will have removed a few scales from your eyes, and you should be able to see more clearly. Ask yourself a few questions.

Are your drinking too much? Sorry, but this is a trap a lot of widows fall into: I know several, especially ones who have been well provided for financially. With no pressures driving them out to work, forcing them to focus on something other than themselves, and with no one suffering economically if they spend too much money on booze, they wallow in self-pity and whisky. And most of their friends are too soft-hearted to tell them to snap out of it. Indulgence is not always kind; self-indulgence is downright destructive. Drinking alone and too much is an unproductive activity. You're being a damn fool if that's what you're doing. Stop it.

Quit drinking. Get a job. Go read to a shut-in. Take a trip. Clean your own house. Have a grandchild. Take a Great Books Course. Have an affair!

Which brings us to the next hard question. Are you screwing around? Are you getting known as an easy lay? Are you being, in other words, promiscuous? In Bermuda, there is an expression for this kind of behaviour, which is often characteristic of frantic, frightened widows. It's called "going foolish." Everyone knows you're not in your right mind, but at least try to hang on to your body. Don't go foolish.

Widows are highly vulnerable. I'll be the first to admit that. It's all too easy to drift in and out of one affair after the other, searching for love and picking up a little easy loving. There are a lot of lonely people out there, willing to be partners. And your friends, if they realize what you're doing, will continue to be kind. They'll forgive you, or refuse to judge you in the first place, and point instead to what you've been through, poor dear. You're going to have to be your own judge.

You think you have nothing left to lose, but you have. It's called self-respect. Decide what you want most, then figure out what to do about it.

There are four kinds of relationships, according to psychologists, that mitigate against loneliness. The first is the romantic sexual relationship. If you can rule that one out, at least for the time being, there are still three others that you can work on. These are friendships, family relationships, and personal commitment to a cause, a course of action, a community, a productive type of work, or a social network of some kind. All these are other-directed. Once you have truly learned to love yourself you can turn your capacity for love, tenderness, care, and concern toward others. And you'll make more friends, almost more than you'll have time for; I guarantee it!

There is a difference between loneliness and being alone. Being alone can get to be a habit, a delightful one. Being alone can give you freedom to do what you want; call it self-indulgence if you will. Being alone can encourage self-development and self-reliance as well, both valuable attributes to have. But an attack of loneliness is an assault on your whole system and on the whole careful structure of self-protectiveness you have set up. Though it may occur less and less frequently as time passes, when an attack does come on, like a tidal wave, the shock can carry you gasping and breathless and sobbing right back to the beach where you were first stranded.

First of all, be comforted; it happens to every widow. Next, what are you going to do about it? All your hard won strength has got to be of some use to you now when you need it. In this list-happy, pragmatic world we live in, there are lots of things you can do about it. Consider:

1. Make a list. Write down the times when your loneliness strikes and take measures to prevent the next attack. Frequently it's seasonal and you can't do much about it. Anniversaries, birthdays, Christmas, Thanksgiving, private milestones in your life together – these can trigger attacks year after year. Widows who become grandmothers long after their husband's death tell me that the birth may cause retroactive pain. I find weddings very painful. As I say, there's not much you can do about something as inexorable as the calendar, except maybe brace yourself, and know that this, too, will pass.

But there are other lists you can make, happier ones. Make a list of dinner parties you'd like to have and list the people you'd invite and plan the menus. You may get around to one or none of them but you've had the time-consuming pleasure of planning them. Make a list of all your clothes, from memory, and then make a list of ones you should get rid of and ones you can add something to so that they'll last another season. Make a list of new clothes you'd like to buy. Now make a list of clothes you can afford to buy! You can make Christmas shopping lists in July if you really get going. Once you get the hang of it, you don't need me to help you.

2. Paint a room, or a piece of furniture, or a picture.

3. Clean your oven.

4. Polish the silver.

5. With everything so clean, have a party!

6. Cook up a storm – for your party.

7. But if you can't afford to have a party, try cooking something you've never cooked before, something really complicated and creative. Even if you don't feel like eating it when you've done, you had the fun and concentration of doing it.

8. Sew something spectacular. For me it's spectacular if I sew on a button, but I know women who enjoy the challenge of a French couturier design pattern.

9. Do something you've never done before. Make it something you've always had a secret desire to do. Obviously there are financial limitations to this. It isn't likely you can take off on a trip around the world. But maybe you've always been meaning to explore an art gallery and never got around to it. Or take in a local ferry boat ride, or train ride, or some equally obvious local tourist attraction that natives never get around to doing. Do it.

10. Take a trip. Invite yourself somewhere. You must have had friends invite you to come and visit. Take them up on it. You needn't stay long. But a visit with friends will give you a real lift and is guaranteed to dispel loneliness.

11. Write something: a poem? a letter? a diary? That's best of all. As a writer I am addicted to paper, but anyone with a fresh pad of paper and a ballpoint pen can write down what she feels and get it out where she can look at it. That's how Lynn Caine, author of the bestseller *Widow*, which you should read, began to write her book. I find a diary is cheaper than a shrink and it helps to distance the pain a little.

12. Cut your hair, or colour it, or both. Remember that line from Wilde's *The Importance of Being Ernest*? "I hear her hair has turned quite gold from grief." I'm not being as facetious as I sound. Have a facial, a pedicure, a massage. Pamper yourself, in other words. Do something to make yourself feel good, and to feel good about yourself.

13. Turn your electric blanket on high and go back to bed. Scunge. One widow wrote me that she used to watch the TV Guide and when there was a movie she really wanted to see on the Morning Movie, she would take a breakfast tray back to bed with her and watch it. Why not?

14. Take a course. Join a political party and work for

it actively. Read a book. You may pamper your body but you should give your mind a good work-out. Take your mind off your troubles and set it other problems.

15. But give your body a work-out, too. Take up a new sport, or go back to an old one. Take tennis lessons. Start jogging. Swim a mile.

16. Make love. This has its complications and drawbacks, which we have already discussed.

17. Get out of the house. Go to a movie or a singles bar (drink pop if you're nervous). Go on a picnic. Take an historic walk. Go to a concert. Explore something.

18. Crawl into a hole and pull the hole in after you. Sometimes it's so bad that's all you can do. Well, go ahead and brood. Wallow in it. Cry. Feel sorry for yourself. But don't try to share this with anyone. When you're fit for human companionship again, emerge, like a butterfly from a grubby cocoon. Have a hot bath – with bubbles – and you're bound to feel better in half an hour.

19. Scream.

20. Pray.

21. Forgive someone. There's a lot of residual anger flying around in you. When you're in one of these moods pick out someone you really feel resentful of and forgive him or her. Do something for her: bake her a loaf of bread or invite her for lunch or write her a note. Freed of even a fraction of your burden of anger, you will feel much much better.

22. Make fudge with a child. If you don't have one the right age, borrow one.

23. Get organized. Getting organized takes a lot of time and can usually get you involved enough to tide you over an attack. You can organize your files – you must have files of something you want organized! Sort out your recipes. Save things. Throw things out. Go through all your magazines. Clip things. Write things down. Oh, this will make you feel better!

24. Start a clippings collection: happy or comforting or challenging, poems, quotations, thoughtful letters from people, news items, encouraging words, cartoons, whatever. Paste them in a scrapbook. Then when you're down you can re-read them. That's why people hang posters like one I found which reads:

I believe in the sun
Even when it is not shining
I believe in love
Even when I am alone
I believe in God
Even when He is silent.

25. Go through it. You have to, you know. There's no turning back.

You will have realized, going through this list, that most of the solutions assume a certain amount of energy on your part. What happens if the spirit is young but the flesh is aging and weak? Loneliness is a problem compounded by age. It takes get-up-and-go to make loneliness get up and go. And sometimes it takes money too, more money than you have. There must be ways that an older person can find to ease the bad days without it costing an arm and a leg, or using tired ones. What can you do?

If society tends to ignore widows generally, it especially neglects older ones, trapped by frailty in a lonely room. Unoccupied time hangs heavy, and you are the one who must fill it, moment by moment, day by day.

I know a woman, a widow, who is trapped by arthritis in a room where she is brought three not-always-inspired meals a day. People who visit her come away with a lift, and so they go back again. She listens to them; she doesn't complain about her own aches and pains, which are myriad and severe. She remembers their children's names, and their husbands', and asks after them. She is glad to see them when they come and never never refers to how long it's been since she saw them last, if indeed it was a long time. She appreciates whatever is done for her and makes her visitor and benefactor feel like a queen for being so gracious and kind and generous. She makes it very easy for people to love her. They want to see her again, so they do.

That woman is my mother.

I am not a TV addict myself, in fact, I rarely watch television, but I bless it daily for the pleasure it brings my mother and all shut-ins. I don't know what Mother would do without her TV families, all the people in the soaps in whose lives she gets involved, to say nothing of the hockey and football games she gets so excited about.

And she does crossword puzzles and double acrostics until they're coming out of her ears. Some women knit; my mother puzzles. She has a mind like a steel trap. I guess I can face pain and aging, failing health and weakening flesh. ("Old age," wrote an aunt of mine, "is not for sissies.") But God grant me my wits. And you yours.

You haven't lived all this time for nothing. You have a few foxy things you can still do. If you can't get out and see the world, then you can get the world to come and see you.

Most centres have mobile library services, which include taking books to shut-ins. If you can't get to the library, ask the library to deliver. If you still enjoy reading, you get a bonus, but even if you don't or just want to look at the pictures, at least you have a human being coming to you – bearing books. And if you're blind, the library will bring you tapes of books to listen to, and a cassette player to listen to them. This service is also available by mail in smaller centres through the CNIB.

If you have a faith, and most people do, whether or not it bears the title of a religion, you can pray a lot. But if you believe in organized religion as well, you're ahead of the game. Make sure your name is still on the lists of whatever church or temple you belonged to, keep up your dues (offering), and you'll be on the visiting list. That means that once or twice or several times a year some of the more active women of the church will bring you flowers left over from a special service or tea, and the minister might even drop in to check on your spiritual progress – and that all makes for more visitors to darken your doorstep and lighten your life.

Enquire about physiotherapy treatments. You probably need them, anyway. Ask your doctor if he would recommend them. A young physiotherapist coming in once or twice a month can do wonders for your morale as well as your muscles and it doesn't cost you anything. She (he?) is paid by whatever form of medical insurance applies to your province and your age.

Similarly, if you're too weak to wash your own hair now, or need some other specific personal help, you can put in for a Victorian Order Nurse to come on a regular basis to help you out – once or twice a week. The charge for this is nominal and varies according to your ability to pay. And it pays off in more than just a clean head. You'll make another young friend and that's always a pleasure.

If you want not only a clean head but a stylish one, check with your local hairdressing association. The Ontario Hairdressers' Association, as an example, has a service now for hospitals, homes for the aged, special-care patients, and senior citizens in private homes. For reasonable prices, you can get a shampoo, a styled haircut, or a permanent from a professional hairdresser. Ask about it and maybe you'll get a new head and a new friend.

Here's another suggestion, one so simple you'll laugh. Write letters. Don't laugh. If your hands aren't too sore, if you can spell, and even if you can't, pick up your ballpoint and write. Write away for things. Get free samples. It'll make your mailbox interesting. Write your MP; he/she has to answer – and you don't have to put a stamp on that letter. Write complaints or kudos to manufacturers. They'll answer too, and probably send you more free samples. Find a pen pal. And, of course, if you have distant children and other relatives, be such a good correspondent that if you were playing tennis you'd beat them hollow, the ball is back in their court so fast. Sooner or later, they'll respond, even sons.

All these are things you can do to keep the world coming to you without stirring out of your room. If you have more than a room, and a little more energy, issue some invitations. By this time you know when the bad times are. Reach out to others then. Share a seasonal downer with them and turn it into a high spot. Beat the Anniversary Reaction. Phone a senior citizen's home, if you aren't in one yourself, and invite two or three of the more active women to join you in your kitchen to bake Christmas cookies, or Easter or Hanukkah bread, or whatever. If you can't afford the price of all the ingredients, ask them to chip in. They'll love the chance to putter in a real kitchen again and to have some home-baking to take back to share with their friends, and you have solved another day of the blahs. You can also do this with your grandchildren, should you be so lucky as to (a) have any (b) in the same city or town. But don't expect their mothers to be pleased with the kid's greasy clothes and full tummies when they return home. Grandmothers are notorious for being a bad influence – I think it skips a generation.

Go back to the piano you're sorry you neglected when your parents nagged you to go and practice; read all the books you never had time to get around to; learn a foreign language; take up painting, and think of

Grandma Moses! Your work is over. Why not give your-self a treat? In doing so, you are doing yourself and the society you live in the biggest service of all. *You are asserting your right to be here.* In her book *The Second Sex* Simone de Beauvoir deals uncompromisingly with the problem of age for a woman. "When she has given up the struggle against the fatality of time," writes de Beauvoir, "another combat begins: *She must maintain a place on earth.*"

You have to keep on having goals in sight. You were not meant to languish in apathy. God grant you your health and your wits and enough money to keep food on your table and a roof over your head so you can keep on truckin'.

It's never too late, as the saying goes. You need not only spirit and wit and means, you need enough *anger* not to let anyone do you in, let you down, put you off, rub you out. In the old days this anger was, I believe, called backbone. It's backbone that is going to give you the strength to keep on doing your own thing. Heaven knows you have the freedom. This is one of the ironies of widowhood, all along the way, that you have been granted unique freedom.

"Strange that creatures without backbones have the hardest shells," wrote the poet Kahlil Gibran. *You* have backbone, so don't bother acquiring a shell. Stay soft. Stay open. Hang loose, as they say. Don't harden with resentment or self-pity. Don't tyrannize other people with your needs. Don't blackmail your children with your love. A free gift of love is infinitely more valuable. Wait for it. You have all the time in the world.

That's what I keep telling myself. I have all the time in the world, and I do. By the time I'm eighty-five, my marriage is going to seem like an interlude in my life, occupying, as it will have, less than one-quarter of it. There are a lot of women like me; some 37 per cent of the widowed in Canada, in fact, are widowed when they have at least half, if not more, of their adult lives left to live. By the same token, 63 per cent of widows are over the age of sixty-five and, life expectancy statistics being what they are, they still have some living to do, too.

According to insurance tables a woman's life expectancy is now about seventy-six years. The average age of widowhood is fifty-six. So the years stretch on ahead, like a long tunnel of time, and what are you going to do with them? After the children have left, after you have retired from your work, and after other women friends have joined your ranks (Welcome to the Club), there remains your own cycle of days to put in before your time is up. Sooner or later, most of us will be aging lonely widows. You can't argue with statistics. The question is: do you have the means to cope with this last challenge life is throwing at you? By "means", I include everything: physical, mental, spiritual, and financial.

You have proved your dogged endurance, your stamina, your innate sense of timing, and your skill at long distances. As you get older why not enjoy it? By this time you have earned a right to your knobs, your nonconformities. You don't have to diet any more – at least not for appearance's sake, though you must guard your health. You can be outspoken and opinionated and eccentric – as long as you remain nice enough to retain your visiting privileges.

"Want to have some fun on your next birthday?" reads a contemporary card. "Paint racing stripes on your cane." I hope this has supplied the paint.

10

Sympathy, haircuts and assorted problems

*What is the world to a man whose wife
is a widow?*

Irish Proverb

People have odd attitudes towards the bereaved, almost
as odd as their attitudes towards death. They attend the
funeral and bury both halves of the couple – or seemingly so. The sight of a recent widow seems to be too
much of a reminder of mortality so they try to avoid her.
When they do run into her, usually by accident and not
by design, they are oversolicitous about her health. They
tell her how fine she is looking.

She isn't. She looks like death warmed over. She
hasn't started to eat or sleep with any regularity yet.
How can she look like anything but what she is – a lost
soul? I could tell when I really started looking better.
People stopped telling me I was looking better.

"You're looking better?" they kept saying hopefully,
with a question. As if you'd been sick. And of course
you were, sick to your soul.

You have suffered one of the most traumatic blows it

112

is possible to suffer. You may be walking around upright but your mind is still on crutches. Well, don't blame people. I've done the same thing myself, both before and since my husband's death. There is something awe-inspiring, silencing, and shattering about emotional pain that does leave one at a loss for words. Perhaps gestures are better. I've mentioned before my need for hugs. I'm sure other people feel the same way. Human physical comfort, no strings. I saw a cartoon once, no caption, which said it all. It was a vending machine; the sign on it read: "Hugs, 25¢." I wish I could have one installed.

It's not that people lack compassion. I do believe that most people think of themselves as kind and well-meaning. They're busy, they're shy, and they're tactless. So maybe if someone told them how to treat a widow, or anyone who has been recently bereaved, it would help us all. And maybe it would also help the bereaved, because they don't always know what they want and wish someone else would figure it out for them.

Listen. Just listen. More than anything, in the first few weeks of horror following a death, the widow needs someone to listen to her. She has to re-live the death, re-live the life she and her husband shared, begin to establish a new relationship with him and with the world she's still living in. She desperately needs to talk. Give her time. Let her talk.

Talk about him with her. Too many people clam up about the dead. It's not going to make her feel worse to talk about him, it's going to make her feel better. Recall funny things he said, nice things he did, good times you had together. My husband was a very witty man. Some of the nicest sympathy letters I received were ones in which the writer recalled some especially witty line he had said.

Conjure up for her the life she had. She has to confront it, look at it, and eventually start to withdraw. Help her to do so. He is still a living presence to her. She'll stop in time. Probably her own good sense will tell her when. One of the really horrible things I did was to talk about my husband on my first dates with other men. Like non-stop. That was hardly fair. It took me a while to realize what I was doing, and then I shut up. It's a test of others' tolerance and good will, I suppose, but it's a wonder they didn't hand me a memorial candle to light and leave.

Invite her over. But don't just say, "Drop in any time," because she won't come. She's feeling hypersensitive and she may have already suffered a few rebuffs or indications that she's not as welcome as she was when she was part of a couple. One of the nicest things any couple did for me was to ask me to their place for a nightcap frequently after choir rehearsal. I used to dread going home at night after a meeting because there was no one to tell about it and the children were in bed. It's something else you have to get used to.

Another couple used to ask me for a TGIF drink on Fridays, and that made me feel as if weekends weren't all bad.

So be specific in your invitations to a widow. Say when. And it wouldn't hurt to make it for dinner once in a while. That applies for months after the fact. If you're feeling guilty because you haven't done anything about poor Mary Smith, it's never too late. She's still alone. Ask her for dinner, preferably on a night when your husband is home. She won't eat him.

Hang in there. So many people, as I have indicated, drift away. Try for a few months, anyway, to give her some regular time. Maybe you could plan a weekly or monthly shopping excursion, something special, or a visit to an art gallery, or a swim, or a walk in the park – anything, just so it's planned and regular and forces her to think ahead a bit, plan for an event in the future, however simple.

Don't give her unsolicited advice. Don't tell her what to do. Don't make harsh judgements of what she has done. She's supersensitive anyway. If she wants your advice, she'll ask for it. I had one friend, within the week of my husband's death, criticize his insurance provisions for me and my family. What could I do about them then? In any case, they were what we had both agreed upon. We had always planned that I would work if he died early (never thinking that he would), and so we planned for a thin bottom line and spent our money on other things, like travel together. I am grateful for my memories.

Don't save up all the hard luck stories to tell her expecting her to realize that she isn't the only one with problems. She knows that, but she's having enough trouble coping with her own right now. Telling her others doesn't make her feel any better.

I had one friend who, whenever we got together, at one point would nod her head wisely and say sententiously, "There are worse things than death." It was home-truth time, and she wanted me to know how lucky I was that I didn't have a living vegetable tied up to tubes in the hospital, or a human skeleton wasting away with pain in front of my eyes. I know, I know. We are given enough strength, I hope, to bear our own pain. I would not trade with others, nor they with me, in all likelihood. Sufficient unto the day.

Don't say, "You're lucky. You still have your children." It's true, they are blessings. But the widow doesn't feel very lucky and resents being reminded that she still owes a debt of gratitude. She'll come around to it.

Don't say, "He had a long, full life." Not full enough as far as she's concerned, and not nearly long enough. I had one widow, whose husband died at sixty-six, say to me that she felt it was too soon and unfair for him to die so young, forgetting that mine had died at forty-five. Tact takes a lot of practice and we all need it.

Do try to remember whom you're talking to. I ran into one woman in the supermarket shortly after my husband died who started telling me that her husband was away on a business trip and she said, "You know how much you get done when they're away and not underfoot." Yes.

"You're so free-wheeling," exclaimed a friend, commenting on the fact that I had driven myself in and out of Toronto (to a business appointment) in a day. "I wouldn't do that except under duress." Or because there's no alternative.

"You're getting so much thinner," exclaimed the same friend. "I envy you." Envy?

"There's someone you should meet," a friend told me. "She just moved in on the street next to you. You'll have a lot in common. Her husband's dead too." Common denominator?

"I guess the mistletoe isn't much use to you," said a friend at my first Christmas party A.D., "all the men here are married."

Don't say, "Cheer up– maybe next time you'll marry a rich husband." I know one widow to whom this was said at graveside. It was six months before someone said it to me. It's such a classic gaffe, I couldn't believe it was actually being said and I laughed out loud.

Don't ask, right after the interment, if she wants to sell the house. Someone asked my mother during my father's terminal illness. Even vultures have the tact to circle a while before they land.

Don't tell her all your troubles with your husband, with the implication that she's lucky she's well out of it. She'll sympathize with your daily concerns, but she doesn't want a glimpse of husband-wife relations, not for a while.

And don't, don't, tell her how importunate your husband is in the bedroom. I can remember being almost sick with pain when a couple of friends started discussing their husbands' sexual behaviour ("He's at me all the time, never leaves me alone"). That's dirty pool.

And, men (we're back to sex again, I'm afraid), don't figure on giving her a treat. But an arm or a shoulder in a friendly hug is okay.

Try, if you can, to remember anniversaries, or at least one milestone in her year. If something aids you in remembering her husband's death date, then write her a note or phone her or send her a rose the following year. She hasn't forgotten what day it is. Or, if you were close, and enjoyed celebrating their wedding anniversary with them, remember it with her. Say something. It won't bring up any pain she might not have experienced. It comforts her that you also miss him and remember the good times.

Remember the good times and the good friends. If I have sounded harsh or critical of some of the treatment I've had, please understand that these were exceptions. As one widow said to me when she found out I was writing a book about widowhood, "Be sure to write about friends." Yes. Where would any of us be without them? I count among my richest blessings the friends who supported and cared for me, and continue to do so, in my loneliness and pain. They think of ways to help me that I could never think of myself. They also think of turning up at moments of need.

And sometimes it's surprising who turns up. The old saying, "You find out who your friends are," is true. Old old friends, of course, remain friends, steadfast and true. But sometimes new friends, people you thought were friends, turn out to have been couple-friends, or convenience-friends, or reciprocal-friends, and when you are no longer part of a couple, when it is no longer convenient to know you, or when you are less able to reciprocate favours or invitations, these people fall away. On the other hand, you will find to your surprise that some of the people whom you thought of as very friendly acquaintances, but not close, become your staunchest supporters and most thoughtful allies. You never know.

One of the most delightful therapeutic things that was done for me happened after I moved to my new home in Toronto. I was invited, by two couples whom I knew well but not intimately, to join their Gourmet Dinner Club. It seems they had suffered several separations in their ranks, and they decided there was as much continuity in a single with a floating partner as there was in a couple with a precarious marriage. I had never recovered my interest in cooking since Bill died. Having to plan menus and suggest recipes to the group, and also, of course, to produce again, was marvellous therapy. It lured me back into the kitchen. Another rule: Help her to find an interest.

Remember that the times when married people are most occupied, widows are probably unoccupied, particularly in the early months. I can remember sitting quietly in my living room early one Saturday evening in June, some six weeks A.D., with soft tears streaming down my face. Someone came whom I didn't know that well, but whom I liked. And we talked. And became better friends.

I remembered the timing and did exactly the same thing for a fresh widow later that fall. And made another friend.

Another time, just before the Stratford Festival opening, which always gives me an Anniversary Reaction, another seemingly remote friend dropped in with some flowers from her garden. And we talked.

If you're too far away to risk a drop-in call, then phone. Say, "Just thought I'd call," and take it from there. You can never go wrong by taking a little thought. And it's never too late. One widow warned me that the second year is in many ways as bad or worse than the first because people think you must be over it by now and withdraw some of their support. She's still alone.

If you're going to a meeting or a dinner or something that you know the widow will be going to as well, ask her if she wants a lift. Sometimes she gets stubborn (I did) and proud and won't ask for help. But she hopes like hell someone else will think of it. I went to my daughter's high school graduation exercises alone because I would not ask to go with anyone, and no one thought of asking me to go with them. I guess that's how I learned to go alone to things. It's either that, or stay at home.

People are wonderful in times of stress. They rally round when there's a death or a serious illness. Then they are kindness itself and they know what to do. But they – we – all tend to forget the dailiness of loneliness and the unrelenting pressure of having to do everything yourself. An occasional thought on a day that isn't special will be greatly appreciated and makes the load seem lighter. Try not to forget her in the daily rush.

A lot of these rules apply to both widow and widower. There are some differences between them and it might help to consider them.

A widow is going to have trouble with maintenance and home repair. If you're a male friend and happen to be handy, ask her if there's anything that needs fixing, or take a look around for yourself. One neighbour of ours noticed that some tiles had dropped off our pool and, without being asked, got some caulking mixture and replaced them. Wow.

A widower, on the other hand, is having trouble coping with the meals. Even if he has very young children and has a housekeeper, you can bet the standards aren't as high as they used to be. Take over a fresh pie, warm from your oven, or a cake, or home-baked bread.

Tell a widower, as tactfully as you can, when his hair needs cutting. Chances are it was his wife who reminded him and she's not around to do it.

Ask him and his family to dinner. This applies to anyone, doesn't it? Breaking bread together is a comforting thing to do. It seems to assert normality, to say, as nothing else does, that life does go on. We all have to eat.

A widower told me he could fix a kettle but he couldn't select his own ties. He can clean the house all right but what's he going to do when a chair needs re-covering, and he can't figure out what colour it should be? He can cook a roast of beef but he can't plan a week's menus and therefore he has trouble with the shopping list.

A widow, on the other hand, has trouble with fuses, car maintenance, and hanging pictures.

Both widow and widower are disoriented, and for much longer than you realize. They go through the motions of normality; they go about what remains of their lives and their business and they seem to be making normal responses to the demands of daily life. But they are only half there. They are conducting a constant inner dialogue with someone who is absent. They are staunching a wound that has torn a gaping hole in their psyches. They are suffering withdrawal symptoms of the most severe kind.

So what can you do? Don't withdraw from them. Give them your support and sympathy. Say you're sorry, and prove it.

11

Plan ahead

A man called on me the other day with the
idea of insuring my life. Now I detest life
insurance agents; they always argue that I
shall some day die, which is not so.

Stephen Leacock

All right, you've been through it. Now, if *you* died last night, would your executor/trix have all the information he/she needed to make life easier for your survivors? Do you, in fact, have an executor? Have you made out a will?

If you were going away on a trip and leaving children behind, you'd leave instructions for the baby-sitter, wouldn't you? Rather complete ones, in fact, with the doctor's phone number, and the numbers of the plumber, TV and washer repair men, and possibly even some suggested menus, and a plan of action. Consider your death, then, merely as a bigger trip with this exception: no one can reach you where you're going. They can't ask you questions then, so answer them before you go.

Few people leave adequate information. Somehow they seem to feel that preparation is like an invitation. It isn't. It's a kindness you can perform for your children or whoever you leave behind. It's not only the financial arrangements that you've made that others have to know about, it's also the fiddley details that no one else knows but you. You might even go so far as to plan your own funeral. I had an aunt who did that. Wrote her own obituary, too.

First the business. Take several sheets of paper and begin your list. You do have a will, don't you? One copy should be with your lawyer and one with you. Write down where it is. (Don't put your will or your life insurance policies in a safety deposit box because it will be sealed on your death and they must be immediately accessible.) List your policies, life, disability, fire, automobile, house, etc., and indicate where they may be found. List your bank accounts and say where your passbooks are. Write down anything, everything you have, bonds, stocks, trust certificates, Registered Retirement Savings Plans, a Registered Home Ownership Savings Plan, deeds, mortgages, contracts, names of any business partners and all papers connected with business arrangements. And tell where they are. Plus your tax returns, financial statements, guarantees and warranties on your possessions (such as stove, car etc.). Where are the car keys and the car ownership registration? Where is the safety deposit box located and where is the key to it?

It would be a very good idea to write down the purchase price of any stocks you own, and the date of purchase, and the maturity dates of bonds, and the expiry dates of guaranteed investment certificates. List your future financial obligations and decisions, such as mortgage payments or stock options. Or tell what your rent is and when it's due. Are there series of post-dated cheques outstanding on that? And make a list of any other post-dated cheques you may have written.

122

Include receipts that would be required to make up your final income tax return, as well as income statements, and don't forget information concerning capital gains or losses. Write down a list of any gifts made, trusts established, charitable gifts (or obligations).

Now list the locations of any stored valuables like jewellery, furs, stamp collections. You might like to talk over with your children the disposition of some of your possessions. Maybe one of them has always secretly loved a particular ornament or painting and would love to have it. Find out now, and reach an agreement about it, verbal or written. Written is better.

List your credit cards and their location, including the duplicates. And don't forget your birth certificate and your Social Insurance card – no one can do a thing without them. Tell where the bills are kept, and list any outstanding debts, including contractual obligations such as cable TV, snow removal contracts, decorating contracts, things on order. List your current and ongoing expenses. List your book club memberships and magazine subscriptions so that something can be done about them. And any club memberships.

Nothing is more baffling than a bunch of keys whose locks are unknown. As a matter of fact, keys paralyze me. I have keys that are meaningless to me now but that somehow I'm afraid to throw away. I have a key that I think belongs to a locker I used when I was at university. If I ever go back in a time machine it could be useful. When I travel I never lock my luggage because I can't identify the keys to any of my bags. I'm not recommending that you harbour unidentified keys. The ideal thing would be to label them. If you're so organized you already have, you don't need to read a list like this.

Tell where your appointment book is and make sure someone will be aware of any appointments you have that have to be cancelled. My husband had just begun a series with a dentist which I had to cancel. Does anyone know similar information about you? You should also have a record of your children's appointments and lessons so that they may be continued (or postponed as the occasion dictates). Do any of your children have a refillable prescription? Where is it? What about their eyes? Where is the correction prescription? Where do you buy their glasses? Where are their birth certificates, passports, school records, medical records? Do any of them have bank accounts or trust funds established for them? Have they had special bequests from grandparents or from your husband that they don't know about? Obviously these questions apply more to younger children, but older ones don't always know everything about themselves, their business and possessions. Are there any insurance policies on them? I take out school insurance on my children each year. If you do that, you'll have to say where those papers are.

If you have any obligations to other relatives, say so. I'm thinking of women who may contribute some support to an aged parent, or who are helping out a child on his own. In the case of the children, the support will likely continue since they will be beneficiaries of any life insurance you may hold, and will inherit your estate. But what about a parent? I am told that it is possible for a widow to buy a contract called a "contingent life annuity" to continue payments to a parent or in-law in the event of your death. It's very cheap because the odds are against your parent outliving you, quite bluntly. The annuity ceases on his or her death and only pays off on yours. This kind of protection can also be arranged for a handicapped sibling or child, but it's much more expensive because the odds are different.

Now start listing names, addresses, and telephone numbers. Start with your lawyer, life insurance agent, casualty agent, accountant, banker, broker, and any other financial advisors you may have. Include your and your children's doctors, dentist, pediatrician, orthodontist, speech therapist – all the people you can think of that you have dealings with. It's a good idea to include the names of teachers, Scout leaders, maybe even a few of your children's close friends. And why not include your maintenance people: plumber, washer repairman, cleaning lady, etc. Who else? Your children know who your friends are, or do they?

Tell them where your Christmas card list is, or your address book, or both. They'll need names and addresses to inform distant relatives (distant geographically, that is) and friends of your death. And a Christmas card list is a handy source of names for pallbearers, if that's the kind of funeral you want. Or you can pick your own pallbearers, and write them down. Include a few alternates, in case some of them go before you do. And while you're at it, include an alternate executor/trix for the same reason. Did you know you can stipulate that your executor receive a fee for services rendered? If you've made a deal with someone to take the chidren, write that down too, though that's probably in your will.

Now a small practical note. Do a quick estimate of what it will cost to settle your estate, pay off the lawyer, any medical bills you may have incurred in your demise, burial fees, etc., and consider taking out a small term insurance policy to look after just these expenses. Term insurance is cheap. A small policy will eliminate a few headaches for your survivors.

One more thing. What about the funeral? Funerals are primitive but they are for the living, not the dead. It took me a while to figure that out. Other people really do need to pay some physical heed to the passing of one from their midst, some nodding of the head, dabbing of the eyes, some salute, some farewell. A funeral with its attendant ritual and ceremony gives the immediate family some opportunity to begin the work of confrontation and withdrawal and provides a social event by which relatives and friends may gather round and offer some comfort for what it's worth. Sometimes it's worth a lot.

Funerals have been much maligned lately. The high cost of dying has been the subject of a great deal of criticism, and ridicule has been hurled at the pussy-footing euphemisms of funeral parlance: The Loved One is resting in The Slumber Room. Satin-quilted caskets and embalming and grave liners are all part of the euphemistic approach to death. They are also part of the emotional blackmail people tend to get caught up in at a time like death. A high-class (read expensive) funeral always costs more than The Departed would have spent.

Funerals have changed very little in format in this century. They're still stuffy and mid-Victorian. When you think how weddings have changed, with the participants writing their own vows, choosing their own blessings, prayers and music, and even location, you realize how backward funerals are. Few people plan their own funerals. Maybe we'd have some better ones if they did. I heard of a memorial service held for a young priest which was a real celebration of his life. People stood up and remembered things about him; tapes were played of the best words from his sermons; the Toronto Dance Company, which he had used in his life for his services, performed at his memorial tribute.

You could do that too, if you planned ahead. I wish I'd thought of some of these things before Bill died.

Since his death, I have discovered that not all the people I once knew are in graveyards. Before, the only one I knew about who wasn't was the poet Pauline Johnson – her ashes are buried in Stanley Park in British Columbia. But here are some other picturesque resting places I have learned since. One friend whose home is beside an artificial lake put her husband's ashes in a thicket of trees on the other side of the lake from the house, all in view of her picture window. The actor Leslie Yeo told me that his wife Hilary Vernon's ashes are under a tree in the lovely farmyard garden of actress Pat Galloway and her husband Dr. Bernhard Frischke. The ashes of Reverend Russell D. Horsburgh are buried in the crawl space under the exact centre of the sanctuary of Zion United Church in Hamilton. There is a plaque on the wall attesting to this fact.

Now why didn't I think of something like that?

As it was, I was very traditional. I was taken to pick a double plot in a Stratford cemetery, and my husband lies on the stage-right side. I bought a large gray marble stone with his name and birth date and death date on it – $500 plus tax. I was reminded of the line "nothing's certain but death and taxes." Very appropriate to tax tombstones. For a little more I could have had my name and birth date put on it – a very popular custom there – all filled out but the last piece of information. I declined, saying I might drown in the South Seas and my body never be recovered, and that would be a terrible waste of stone-cutting. I honestly don't like that empty space waiting for me. Every time one of my kids gets sick I think maybe they'll beat me to that space. That's morbid.

Even during the neuter time of my post-amputative recovery I wrote in my diary: "If I ever marry again, whose wife will I be when I die and where will I be buried?" And the real cruncher is that I'm a terrible gardener. Every time I go and look at the sad geraniums I put in each year and the struggling Japanese yews I planted I say to my husband: "Well, you always knew what a terrible gardener I am."

One widow I know found herself washed up on a more alien shore than mine. She and her four children left Ohio after her husband suddenly died. She knew she would never return. She bought a single plot, one small marker, took a picture of it, and moved back to Canada with her kids.

Bodies take up a lot of space in graveyards. Some big cities and small islands have resorted to stacking. Ecologically speaking, it is very wasteful to stick a body in a piece of ground and do nothing else with the ground, There's a lot to be said for cremation. Unfortunately for me, it wasn't said before my husband died.

If we're going to talk about cremation, why not talk about transplants and the whole medical science of spare parts? Whether the remains are going to be burned or buried, there is no earthly reason why you shouldn't donate any good usable pieces so that others may live. Quite a lot of a human being can be recycled now: the corneas, the kidneys, the heart, and they're talking about the pituitary gland. God knows, you won't be using them where you're going. If you retain some sort of vague idea about the literal resurrection of the body, that's all right, too. You don't have to worry. If Judgement Day really is a literal one-time event (I have a theory about it occurring all the time on a time-warp) with all the people who ever lived all brought together at the same time, the spare parts and the ashes will certainly be reassembled as well. If God can handle the traffic problem, He can do anything, and He *can* do anything. Consider giving your parts to a good cause – another human being.

I wish I had discussed this with my husband, but I can do something about me at least. Why don't *you* take time now and think about it? Think it through. The government of Ontario has made a consent form available to every driver. It's on the back of the driver's licence and has space to indicate what parts you're willing to spare in case of a fatal accident. It's a shame to let them go to waste. You can enquire whether your province has a similar provision or ask what your local hospitals are doing.

Even if you give your body to science or to other people, it won't all be used. The remains still have to be disposed of so you can't get around the problem that way. You still have to decide how to deal with what's left. The average funeral and burial now costs a high of $800 in Ontario and a low of $400 in British Columbia. You can cut a few corners by asking for the cheapest casket, skipping the grave liner, and requesting no embalming, but you may get an argument from the funeral director, especially on the last item.

Viewing the body, I am told, is very important. It begins the grief work for everyone. You have to see it to believe it. But to be seen, the body must be presentable. Therefore it must be embalmed. What if you want a closed casket? Not a good idea, according to funeral directors. Because then, of course, you wouldn't need the embalming.

It is impasses like this that lead one to memorial societies. There are twenty-four memorial societies in Canada with a total membership of 130,000. The societies are non-profit, non-denominational, and, understandably, not too highly regarded by funeral directors. A memorial society will help you to the simplest, most inexpensive form of burial or cremation you want. You could join one now and save your survivors a few more decisions.

If that's what you want. Some people want pomp and panoply. I had an aunt, the one who wrote her own obituary, who demanded the most expensive casket available. She said she'd never had a Cadillac in her lifetime so she wanted a Cadillac of coffins when she died. She got it.

If you are traditionally inclined and want to go through the formal ceremonies of a funeral with all the trimmings – but not too expensive – there is a very good little book in the Self-Counsel series that can help you. It's called the *Canadian Guide to Death and Dying*, and it's by a widow, Jill Watt, who found out the hard way everything you need to know about funerals, science donations, religious practices, estates, and pension plans.

Most people think they're immortal, until it's proved otherwise. This seeming inability to envision one's own death, coupled with a general shrinking from the subject on the part of society at large, leaves most people completely unprepared for death, whether it's sudden or after a prolonged illness. As a matter of fact, in the case of a diagnosed terminal illness, the silence can often be worse. I know several widows and one widower who maintained, by some sort of mutual tacit agreement, complete silence about the impending death of their respective spouses. Neither party was willing to call a spade a spade, let alone acknowledge the imminent need to dig a grave with one.

Death is the only obscenity left in our society, the taboo that everyone still observes. I suppose it's fear of the unknown. But you and I know, don't we?

I'm not afraid of dying and death. It's living that's hard.

12

Help is on the way

God help those who do not help themselves.

Addison Mizner

This is a do-it-yourself age we live in. Books and courses abound in self-help projects ranging from furniture upholstery to self-hypnosis. The magazines and newspapers are full of advice about anything that's troubling you, from dry skin to weekend guests, and they give short courses in everything from dog-training to balancing a budget. Entire bookstores are devoted to nothing but can-do books. There are information services provided by just about every business you can name, with pamphlets available on request, teaching the consumer how to use the product in question. Often the product is information itself. *Chatelaine* magazine publishes a series of Cope-Kits; *The Financial Post* published a series of booklets about money management; the Canadian Life Insurance Association issues any number of informative booklets about insurance, naturally, but also about money management, budget handling, etc. The federal government publishes all kinds of brochures and books on anything you care to name from Canadian wildlife to Canada's Food Rules (can you name them?).

So what?

You might be the most competent person in the whole world, and you certainly know how to read directions, but you can't help feeling paralyzed when it's all laid on your shoulders – everything, all the maintenance, all the decisions, everything. And there are times when you just don't know where to turn, who to ask, how to find the answers you need.

What you need first is the sure and certain knowledge that you are going to survive. It said that in the newspaper, didn't it? "He is survived by his wife." Your back may be against the wall; you may be driven to tears, but you will not be driven to total collapse. And even if you are, well, there's help for that, too.

The few names and addresses and hints I can give you are nothing to the mountains of information and assistance waiting for you. All I intend to do is give you a few signposts, and a lot of reassurance.

Everyone has a different weak spot. I get paralyzed by some things I have to do that I call "fiddleys," time-consuming, annoying, fiddley details that have to be looked after. I have a friend who feels the same way I do. Know what she did? She hired a college student on a part-time basis, so much an hour, to do her fiddleys for her. She spends less on that than she would spend on a cleaning lady, and she doesn't mind cleaning her own house. Her part-time organizer has done things like this for her: renewed her passport, taken inventory of her possessions for insurance evaluation, ordered her children's winter underwear, returned things that aren't suitable (I know this can be done by phone, but it's fiddley). My friend is much more relaxed now.

The most fiddley thing I have to do each year is work on my income tax. It really is fiddley because I am a free-lance writer and my income derives from a lot of different sources. I also have fiddley expenses that must be kept track of, like parking and postage, paper, and books, and typewriter ribbon and all stuff like that. I bought a cheap calculator, at my son's suggestion, to help me put my receipts in order before I go to a tax accountant to help me. Some widows I know say they feel a real thrill of accomplishment when they work out their own income tax forms. I'd go to jail before I achieved that thrill. I choose to use the help available. One tax deduction I might not know about pays for the accountant's services, and his services are deductible, too.

If you have other financial problems, there are experts around to talk to you, besides books and brochures to read, and courses to take. Your banker doesn't charge; maybe he's the one to start with. Talk to a friend's husband who you think is pretty clued in (but don't ask for a private consultation). If you do have to go to a lawyer or a professional consultant, just remember that his rates per hour are high, so do your homework as I do for my accountant. Prepare your material, your questions, your information so that you will use as little of his time as possible in briefing him before you ask your questions. You will be paying him then for his expertise and not for his paperwork.

If you have a job problem, there are people who can help you. I have mentioned the assistance and guidance and training available from Canada Manpower, with its offices located across the country. There are special resources now for women returning to the job market that are well worth looking into. And the Women's Centres in most of the community colleges have people and guidance waiting for you. If you already have a job and are having trouble, go to the personnel officer in the company, or if it's too personal a problem, talk it over with a trusted friend.

What you have to have is a positive attitude. *Of course*, this problem can be solved. *Of course*, you're going to solve it. You solved the last one, didn't you? Each time you solve a problem successfully, it gives you that much more confidence for the next one. That's what I keep telling myself, but someone keeps thinking up new problems!

If you really can't cope, if the world is too much with you and you feel too discouraged and bogged down to carry on, then go to your doctor. But don't accept a course of tranquillizers without attempting a long-term solution to your problem. Treat the cause, not the symptoms. Go to your minister or rabbi, or make an appointment with a counsellor, or get your doctor to refer you to a psychiatrist if things are really bad. It wouldn't hurt to pray, too.

Some organizations and services that a widow may find helpful are self-explanatory and fairly easy to find, such as the Big Brothers organization, or the local chapter of Parents Without Partners. Others defy discovery. Just keep asking questions.

There is a growing movement across the country of self-help programs for widows, but the movement is sporadic and seems to depend on a catalyst or leader to get anything going in any given place. Thus, Elsie Palmer in Vancouver began the LIFE – Living Is For Everyone – program at the Vancouver YWCA, which has been operating successfully for several years. Lawra Hopkins is secretary of a new Association for Widows which has been set up in Victoria, B.C. Joy Saltstone started one in North Bay. A group of Jewish widows in Toronto with sons in the twelve-to-fifteen-year age bracket banded together to help each other over the difficult time of their sons' bar mitzvahs. Another group of widows in Hamilton has begun an association that includes widowers (no more than 1.5 widows allowed per widower!).

The River Heights Family Life Education Centre in Winnipeg ran a course on Grief Recovery at Harrow United Church in the spring of 1976; St. James Bond United Church in Toronto is just starting one. Rev. Donald Parr and a social worker Mrs. Beverley Hurlburt at St. Andrew's United Church, Markham, Ontario, have been running a program entitled Good Grief, repeated about once a year, for several years now.

Maria Kluge started the machinery rolling in Brantford, Ontario, to launch a widow-contact group in co-operation with the local Red Cross. Begun in the spring of 1977, the project should be off the ground by the time this book is published.

And then there is the international self-help group known as THEOS (They Help Each Other Spiritually) with fifty chapters in North America and growing all the time. At present, there is only one in Canada, in Toronto, but the movement is growing rapidly. A grief group with religious orientation, THEOS is designed to help the bereaved, not only widows.

Another self-help group with a similar name but with no affiliation with THEOS started in Glenwood United Church in Windsor in 1976. Louise Allen, Rev. Bob Giuliano, and Sister Mary Fran Gilleran advertised a meeting for widows and widowers, expecting a turn-out of maybe two dozen people. One hundred and forty-four showed up, demonstrating the tremendous need for this kind of support system. If there seems to be nothing available in your community, maybe you are the one to initiate something and so to help others.

Local YWCAs in their various Life Skills courses have been getting into programs for single persons, whether separated, divorced, or widowed. And Family Service Associations across the country try to keep abreast of what is going on at the local level.

Two major projects have emerged, one in Winnipeg,

the other in Toronto. The Widows Consultation Centre was established as a service of the Winnipeg YWCA in 1974 through a grant from The Great-West Life Assurance Company. It was originally modelled after the Widows Consultation Centre in New York, but Diane DeGraves, the director, says, "We were not in business long before we realized that few widows will take the initiative in contacting an agency for help." So they launched a service based on the widow-to-widow program developed by the Harvard Medical School. A similar operation, Community Contacts for the Widowed, began officially in Toronto in the spring of 1976 after a two-year pilot project conducted by the Clarke Institute.

Thus, the churches and Ys and community service organizations across the country are beginning to recognize the need and to take the responsibility for meeting it.

Grief and loneliness are legacies of bereavement which must be faced and coped with. Nothing is quite so difficult when there is sympathy, practical help, a chance to communicate one's feelings, and guidance along the way.

Don't be afraid to ask for help. Yelp and holler a little. Someone will hear.

Bibliography

Beresford-Howe, Constance. *The Book of Eve*. Toronto: Macmillan of Canada, 1973.

Bel Geddes, Joan. *How to Parent Alone*. New York: The Seabury Press, 1974.

Caine, Lynne. *Widow*. New York: William Morrow & Company, 1974.

De Beauvoir, Simone. *The Second Sex*. New York: Bantam Books, 1968.

Edwards, Marie, and Hoover, Eleanor. *The Challenge of Being Single*. Canada: New American Library, 1975.

Gladstone, Bernard. *The New York Times Guide to Home Repair Without a Man*. New York: Quadrangle/New York Times Company, 1974.

Glick, Ira O., Weiss, Robert S., Parker, C. Murray. *The First Year of Bereavement*. New York: John Wiley & Sons, 1974.

Grollman, Earl A., ed. *Explaining Death to Children*. Boston: Beacon Press, 1967.

Harris, Janet. *The Prime of Ms America: The American Woman at 40*. Toronto: Longman, Canada Ltd., 1975.

Jackson, Edgar N. *Telling a Child About Death*. New York: Channel Press, 1965.

Keleman, Stanley. *Living Your Dying*. New York: Random House, 1974.

Kieran, Sheila. *The Non-Deductible Woman*. Toronto: Macmillan of Canada, 1970.

Kubler-Ross, Elisabeth. *Death: The Final Stage of Growth*. New Jersey: Prentice-Hall Inc., 1975.

Lewis, C.S. *A Grief Observed*. London: Faber & Faber, 1961.

Lifton, Robert Jay, and Olson, Eric. *Living and Dying*. New York: Bantam Books, 1974.

Marris, Peter. *Loss and Change*. Garden City, N.Y.: Anchor Press/Doubleday, 1975.

Nelson, Paula. *The Joy of Money*. New York: Stein and Day, 1975.

Porat, Dr. Frieda, with Meyers, Karen. *Changing Your Life Style*. New York: Bantam Books, 1973.

Porter, Sylvia. *Sylvia Porter's Money Book*. Garden City, N.Y.: Doubleday, 1975.

Pincus, Lily. *Death and the Family: The Importance of Mourning*. New York: Vintage/Random House, 1974.

Selye, Hans. *The Stress of Life*. New York, Toronto, London: McGraw-Hill paperbacks, 1956.

Snyder, Christopher. *How to Be Sure to Get the Right RRSP*. Toronto: Marpep Publishing, 1976.

Taves, Isabella. *Women Alone*. New York: Funk & Wagnalls, 1968.

Vogel, Linda Jane. *Helping a Child Understand Death*. Philadelphia: Fortress Press, 1975.

Watt, Jill. *Canadian Guide to Death and Dying*. Vancouver: International Self-Counsel Press Ltd., 1974.

Yates, Martha. *Coping*. Englewood Cliffs, New Jersey: Prentice-Hall Inc., 1976.

You. *The Nothing Book*. Warner Books.

Booklets:
For Widows Only
    write to: Every Woman's Books,
                2033 Oak Bay,
                Victoria, B.C.

The Financial Post Books
    Your Money: How to Make the Most of It
    Money Management Book
    Your Guide to Investing for Bigger Profits

CLIA Booklets
    You and Your Group – on group insurance
    After the Gold Watch – on retirement and pension
    information
    Family Money Manager – budgeting guide

For these and other life insurance information:
    Canadian Life Insurance Association
    Box 2110
    Toronto, Ontario M5W 1H1
    Toll free: 1-800-261-8663 (From British Columbia:
        112-800-261-8663)

Index